EQUILIBRIUM

The *yang* having reached its climax retreats in favor of the *yin;*
the *yin* having reached its climax retreats in favor of the *yang.*

Lao Tzu, *Tao Te Ching*

Books by John Cantwell Kiley

Einstein and Aquinas

Effigies: Verses (1956-70)

Robins for Rebecca: Animal Verses

Elementary, My Dear Buckley: A Verse Entertainment

Bumbleberry Tales: A Prose Entertainment for Children

Self-Rescue

Incunabula: Poems

Your Erroneous Bones: A Spoof

Equilibrium

Your Inside Job: A Manual (forthcoming)

Rapping Up the Seventies: A Verse Entertainment (forthcoming)

The Gates of Hell: An Eschatological Novel (in progress)

EQUILIBRIUM

JOHN CANTWELL KILEY

GUILD OF TUTORS PRESS
Los Angeles

FIRST EDITION

10 9 8 7 6 5 4 3 2 1

Library of Congress Catalog Card Number 79-54813

ISBN: 89615-022-4

Designed by Paul O. Proehl

Acknowledgments

Grateful acknowledgement is made to the following for permission to reprint material copyrighted or controlled by them:

Selections from "The People of Tao Chou" in *Translations from the Chinese* by Arthur Waley. Copyright 1941 by Arthur Waley. Printed by permission of Alfred Knopf, Inc. Selections from "Now Does Our World Descend," by E.E. Cummings, "Misery," by John Holmes and "The Falls," by F.D. Reeve in *The New Yorker Book of Poems*. Reprinted by permission of Viking Press. Selections from *The Way of Zen* and from *The Two Hands of God* by Alan W. Watts. Copyright 1958 and 1963 by Alan W. Watts. Reprinted by permission of Pantheon Books, a division of Random House, Inc. Selections from "In a Dark Time," by Theodore Roethke and from "Credibility," by John Ciardi in *Today's Poets*, edited by Chad Walsh. Copyright 1972 by Theodore Roethke and John Ciardi. Reprinted by permission of Charles Scribner's Sons. Selection from the *Myth of Sisyphus* by Albert Camus. Copyright 1955 by Albert Camus. Printed by permission of Alfred Knopf, Inc. Selection from *God's Images* by James Dickey. Copyright 1977 by James Dickey. Printed by permission of The Seabury Press. Selection from "Little Gidding," in *The Four Quartets*. Copyright 1943 by T.S. Eliot. Printed by permission of Harcourt Brace Jovanovich, Inc. Selection from *Delusions, Etc. of John Berryman*. Copyright 1972 by The Estate of John Berryman. Printed by permission of Faber and Faber, Ltd. Selections from *Self Portrait in a Convex Mirror: Poems by John Ashbery*. Copyright 1976 by John Ashbery. Printed by permission of Penguin Books. Selections from *Mind and Nature* by Gregory Bateson. Copyright 1979 by Gregory Bateson. Printed by permission of Dutton & Co., Inc. Selections from "The Road Less Traveled," by Robert Frost, edited by Louis Untermeyer in *Robert Frost's Poems*. Copyright 1977 by Robert Frost. Printed by permission of Pocket Books, Inc. Selections from *The Snow Leopard* by Peter Matthiessen. Copyright 1978 by Peter Matthiessen. Printed by permission of The Viking Press. Selection from "Crazy Jane and the Bishop," by W.B. Yeats in *The Collected Poems of W.B. Yeats*. Reprinted by permission of Macmillan Publishing Co., Inc. Selections from *Common Sense Suicide* by Doris Portwood. Copyright 1977 by Doris Portwood. Printed by permission of Dodd, Mead & Company.

CONTENTS

For William Ernest Carlo
(1921 — 1971)
Philosopher, Teacher, Friend
He was a verray parfit, gentil knight

FOREWORD

This is the second book of a trilogy, Jack Kiley tells us. And, indeed, its close relationship with the first book, *Self-Rescue*, is evident. The basic concepts are the same. The books are hardly the same, however. In each, the concepts are fleshed out and applied in different manners. *Self-Rescue* was a good book; this is an even better one.

What are the basic concepts? For this you must read the book. Jack Kiley is an excellent writer of prose as well as a respected poet, and the basic concepts he is trying to teach us are ones from the discipline of philosophy — and particularly from that branch of philosophy known as ontology or the study of being.

This is not some philosophy or ontology textbook in the ordinary sense. For one thing, it is far too well written. For another, Kiley's motive is not to teach us dry philosophy *per se* but rather how to use philosophy to live well — to live with openness and freedom, with health and wholeness. It is for this reason he can describe himself properly as a clinical philosopher.

This is neat stuff. In my own work, I am devoted to achieving a cooperation, an integration, between psychiatry and religion. And there is plenty of room for philosophers on the healing team. There has been too much specialization. In applying philosophy to the healing of unnecessary hurt and bad habits of thinking, Kiley is not only striking a blow against excessive specialization of the "helping professions" but also making original contributions to the body of theory and understanding about mental illness.

Moreover, at least some of his ideas actually work! *Self-Rescue* is, among other things, the most truly helpful book I know for people struggling to free themselves from addictions of any kind. And this book, among many other things, offers enormous consolation to anyone facing death or dealing with "disaster." It teaches us much about keeping our balance, our sense of humor. It even teaches us, if we are willing to learn, what Herman Hesse in *Steppenwolf* termed "cosmic humor."

I do not mean to imply that I agree with everything Jack Kiley has to say. In his introduction to *Self-Rescue*, William F. Buckley, Jr., aptly described Kiley as a "giant, red-bearded leprechaun," and then went on to say, "But I would like to enter a small reservation. Namely, that he is wrong." I disagree with Mr. Buckley. I do not think that Kiley's basic theology and ontology are all wrong. But I do not think they are all right, either. Kiley has a major vision of the way things are, but I do not think his vision is complete. I am not sure that any ordinary human's vision can ever be complete. Perhaps Thomas Aquinas's was when, near death, he proclaimed that all his great penetrating theological writings were "so much straw."

Dr. Kiley is a missionary. He has had a vision and he is out to sell us on it. And I am glad that he is doing so, because it is a profoundly useful vision — one to which we need exposure. But like almost every missionary and every writer (one has to be a missionary of sorts to be a good writer), he tends to assume that his vision is complete and all-encompassing, the one and only true faith, so to speak, instead of but a single point of view, accurate as far as it goes, but not the whole story. It is because of this single-mindedness that he seems to me occasionally to err, particularly when he attempts awkwardly to fit certain phenomena into his vision when they can be better understood by a different, but also valid, frame of reference. His handling of the phenomenon of repression is a case in point.

So I urge the reader to approach Jack Kiley as one does a missionary: with a certain amount of skepticism. But do not be put off by my reservations. Because the first part of that sentence reads, "I urge the reader to approach Jack Kiley." Do not run away from him. Do not run away from him because he is a missionary, or because he is a philosopher, or because he believes in God. Instead approach him. He has some very valuable things to say, and we can learn from him.

Equilibrium is a highly worthwhile book. Some of the quotes and epigraphs he has selected are themselves worth the price of the volume. But its essence is much more than clever quotations. Nor is it simply a self-help book for the sophisticated (although it is that also). It is a serious work which should be read by the serious seeker. Not because the reader will discover all the answers here, but because he or she will thereby become a more competent seeker. Jack Kiley may not have reached all the answers, but he clearly asks the most important questions, which is no mean feat. We are dealing here with issues of God and atheism, of mysticism and materialism, of death and afterlife, of reality and illusion, of beauty and emptiness, of sanity and insanity. *Equilibrium*, in the words of one of its chapter titles, eloquently concerns itself with "what *really* matters."

M. Scott Peck, M.D.
New Preston, Connecticut

INTRODUCTION: THE INTERNAL RESPONSE

In one and the same sky the poet may discover the habitation of angels, whilst the sailor sees only a promise of dirty weather ahead.

— Evelyn Underhill

If you are like everyone else of a certain age in this world, you are no stranger to disappointments, setbacks, and losses in your life. Each human life has its share of miseries — some more, some less. Yet the seriousness of the dark event is not a simple matter of its kind or intensity; otherwise everyone would be affected alike by the discovery of an irreversible illness, the breakup of a marriage, the loss of a loved one. The evidence is abundant that they are not. The difference in human suffering can only be finally accounted for by the internal response to an event, not by the event itself.

We will be concerned in the pages that follow not with changing the facts of your life, but with your way of looking at them. For the word "fact" has no absolutely independent meaning, that is, apart from your point of view. And this is equally true of the so-called "hard" facts.

You may ask: What can I do about the fact that I am forty or eighty? Plenty. A recent best-selling book had the title *How Did I Get To Be Forty and Other Atrocities?* and illustrates in a few words what I mean. The way you get to be forty is by living forty years, something of an achievement when you consider how many never make it to that age.

This book will stick sedulously to the facts about common human experience, but will invite you to repeated changes in understanding that will give these facts a new meaning. For facts do not "speak for themselves." Not really.[1] *They speak only when spoken to by the understanding intelligence.*

There is an ancient Chinese poem that illustrates better than any words of mine this simple yet important truth. It was written by Po Chu-i in the early Ninth Century.

> In the land of Tao-chou
> Many of the people are dwarfs;

The tallest of them never grow to more than three feet.
They were sold in the market as dwarf slaves and yearly
    sent to court;
Described as "an offering of natural products," I never heard
    of one yet
That parted men from those they loved, never to meet again!
One day Yang Ch'eng came to govern the land;
He refused to send up dwarf slaves in spite of incessant
    mandates.
He replied to the Emperor, "Your servant finds in the Six
    Canonical Books
'In offering products, one must offer what is there, and not
    what isn't there.'
On the waters and lands of Tao-chou, among all the things
    that live
I find only dwarfish *people;* no dwarfish slaves."
The Emperor's heart was deeply moved and he sealed and
    sent a scroll:
"The yearly tribute of dwarfish slaves is henceforth annulled."

The people of Tao-chou,
Old ones and young ones, how great their joy!
Father and son and brother with brother henceforward kept
      together;
From that day for ever more they lived as free men.

      The people of Tao-chou
      Still enjoy this gift.

And even now when they speak of the Governor
Tears start to their eyes.
And lest their children and their children's children should
      forget the Governor's name,
When boys are born the syllable "Yang" is often used
      in their forename.[2]

Notice that there was no change in the so-called "facts" of the situation, in the hard reality of it; the little people remained just what they were: little people. There was an important change, however, in the way the Emperor *viewed* them — and perhaps even in the way the little people viewed themselves.[3] The Governor knew that slaves were not "out there" like trees and goldfish, aided as he was by the Six Canonical Books. He took a grave risk: could he be sure that the Emperor knew it, too? Heaven, as the Chinese say, smiled on him.

Were you the personal beneficiary of Governor Yang's enlightenment, you would not have had to wonder how a better understanding of the fact of your physical stature would benefit you, free you from misery, unpaid toil, and danger.

Yet you need not wait for some wise Governor or Emperor — or anyone else — to discover you. It is nice when they do. It is also rather rare. You are not in control of the views of your fellow human beings; nor are you responsible for those views. You are, however, the custodian of your own views, most importantly, of your own view of yourself, producing them in the inner forum of your own mind.

Some people have only the dimmest awareness of this fact and, when it is pointed out to them, sometimes react with amazement, disbelief, and even shock. The hearing that their views of reality — including that of themselves — are self-produced, that is to say, mental states that have no reality unless and until created in their own consciousness, is startling to them. This is understandable: if true, it means genuine self-autonomy, freedom and . . . responsibility — with all its resulting implications in life.

It is the exact purpose and aim of this book to help you discover this marvelous truth about your own existence. What truth? *That you and you alone are responsible for your own happiness — or lack of it.* That the way you manage your consciousness — beginning now — will decide your fate. Nobody else, nothing else, can be blamed for it.

First you must discover that you are real, that you are not reducible to any human category, even to one of your own making. And, because you are real, you are in most intimate relationship with the universe. As the name suggests, you are one *(uni)* with it. Because you are real, any categorization of you proposing to you that *this* is what you *really* are, is necessarily a distortion of you and a danger to you. Simply put, you are not a category of mind; you are not even what you think you are.

You are beyond categories. You are real with the reality of the universe itself.

The book is entitled *Equilibrium.* Isn't this just another category? Certainly it is a category of thought, yet it is more than that: It is a real state of existence. And so central to our understanding of reality, that we will examine it in the first chapter.

Let us get on, then, with our project.

Chapter 1
A LOOK AT EQUILIBRIUM

*Thou canst not stir a flower
Without troubling a star.*

— Francis Thompson

Every mind, just like every part of the existing universe, enjoys its own equilibrium. The thinker experiences this equilibrium as mental consistency, as the state of the coherence of his thoughts and their integration into his whole system of thoughts. The maniac, for example, never thinks *he's* crazy, however much he believes the rest of the world is. Yet there is always in him some awareness, however dim, however obscured by the glare of thought, that he is not well, that he is dangerous, that he needs help. This is an incursion of the wider consciousness of the knower and his intellect into the mind's scenario, an incursion which the mind tends more or less passionately to resist. The basis of this resistance is the mind's internal sense of consistency[1] of its ideas, of equilibrium, a sense which the mind, as author, is prepared to defend against any challenge coming from without.

The mind, of itself, cannot know its own equilibrium, however. The reason for this is that the mind cannot be aware of itself directly. If the mind were to cease for a moment to do what it does, to *think*, there would be (a) nothing for it to discover, and (b) nothing with which to discover it. The mind is an invention of intellect which, together with the will, are the two components of human intelligence. The mind comes into existence when the intellect turns from knowing the world outside itself to reflecting on its own contents. This causes mental *beings* to arise in consciousness which can be called, loosely speaking, "thoughts."

Equilibrium is defined as the state of balance or rest due to the equal action of opposing forces.[2] Another definition calls it "mental balance." Applying these definitions, must we conclude that the mind of the maniac lacks mental equilibrium? Not at all. Every mind, being real, is always essentially in balance.

Yet surely, you say, there are states of reality, physical states, for example, which are so out of balance that it takes an earthquake to restore them. The earthquake is only the rather showy display of sound and geological effects accompanying an essentially noiseless and continuous process. Let me illustrate this: Picture a great pyramid of rock which rests not on its broad base but on its apex. It is in exquisite but precarious balance. Now let some faint wind, some child's fingertip enter the scene of this neat equilibrium, and our pyramid immediately comes crashing down. In all the noise and excitement it is easy to suppose that some great imbalance took over. Not so. What happened was this: The perceptually neat balance of the pyramid was succeeded by a host of less discernible, smaller states of balance. At no time was anything real "out of balance:" Imbalance is one of those negativities (like darkness, blindness, cold, etc.) which have no real existence in themselves.

And so it is with mind, including the mind of the maniac or the psychotic. The mind of anyone is always real. I do not mean that it is real the way the brain or intellect or will is real; the mind is a moment by moment invention of the intellect, i.e., it is the intellect engaged in thinking. Thinking is just one of the intellect's many cognitive activities, including sensing, imagining, remembering, knowing by conception, knowing by intuition, conscious and unconscious awareness. Thinking reveals the intellect's ability to reflect on its own contents — on its own images and concepts — and to transform them into ideas. Ideas are concepts cut loose from their connection with the objective world. Once this has been done, ideas become true mental entities, for they now have *only* a mental existence, an existence which derives from and depends upon mental activity. In this sense thoughts or ideas are creations of mind, more properly, productions or "fictions."[2]

It must not be supposed that fictions are not real. They are very real. The person who flings himself off the Golden Gate bridge is not in flight from nothing but from some definite reality. Yet for all that, the suicide is really in flight from his thoughts — or, more accurately, from the pain which such thoughts give him. It is not the unbearability of the world but the unbearability of his *perception* of it which prompts the suicide's trip to and over the bridge rail.

If the psychotic's mind is in equilibrium no less than the healthy person's, it may be asked: What is the difference between them?

The psychotic consciousness has been "captured" by the mind. It is as though, to use an illustration from an earlier book,[3] Huckleberry Finn had entered the library of Mark Twain, tied up his creator and carted him off to his raft for a trip down the Mississippi of the mind. In this capture, consciousness has been drawn tightly into itself by mind, so that its contact points with the world outside thought have been reduced to an absolute minimum. It stands, as it were, like an inverted pyramid, touching the "ground" of the objective world only at the point of the apex. It lacks the broad stability of the healthy mind, which is solidly connected at many points of its base with the outside world. The psychotic's mind has internal equilibrium, a consistency binding all its fictions into a coherent mass, but is unstable relative to the "ground," to the objective world. This instability is indicated by the irrational behavior of the psychotic, his susceptibility to being overturned by faint provocation or trauma.

These public signs of behavior are the only way the psychotic's condition can be known clinically. His mind, like the mind of the sane person, remains private and hidden. If the psychotic vocalizes an unease about himself, it is never about the consistency of his system of ideas but about its "fit" with the objective world he glimpses only in flashes, if at all. Neither the psychotic nor the sane person knows the condition of his mental health by any scanning of his mind for mental consistencies or coherencies. Every mind enjoys its own particular internal equilibrium[4] or, to put it more correctly and revealingly, every mind *is* its own equilibrium. This means that each mind always has a reassuring sense, as mind, that it is self-consistent.

It is by means of behavior, by external evidence, that the internal "shape" or configuration of a mind is revealed — whether and to what degree consciousness is being "captured" by mind. And this is just as true for the subject possessing the particular consciousness and mind as it is for his public. A person must wait to see how he acts in concrete circumstances really to know what "shape" his mind is in. He cannot tell by any direct glimpse into his mind or consciousness, by any test of the equilibrium of his ideas. He always encounters equilibrium because, like everyone else, he is an expert at rationalizing his ideas, always hard at work fabricating ideas which serve to balance other ideas in his mind.

The rationalizing activity which goes on continuously in every mind, whether sane or psychotic, is a powerful response to the instinct for wholeness, for integrity, for self-unity. Just as everyone flees instinctively any physical injury which would threaten his integrity, there is a similar continuous effort within the mind to maintain wholeness, to repel all ideas which are not hospitable to earlier basic ideas which have been permanently adopted as truly one's own. Such basic ideas, which may have been imposed in childhood, or worked out consciously in the lessons of experience, tell the person who he *really* is, define for him the very essence of his moral being.

This does not mean that his basic self-definition is true. More than likely it is false, a mere caricature of what he really is, a fundamental misreading of his true nature. Yet to him it is true, and not because it has been proved by the weight of evidence to his intellect, but because it has been *assumed* to be true by some deep, fatalistic temptation of his heart. His is a kind of primordial recognition not just of a fact but of a role he must play, a role he somehow wants to play and has the aptitude and zest to learn quickly. What the author Saul Bellow said about himself: "Asking me what I might have been besides a writer is like asking an earthworm what else he considered becoming," can, with different wording, be spoken with as much sincerity by everyone. Both moralists and psychologists know that if the professional criminal's self-image cannot be changed, any attempt at change will be cosmetic. And what is true for the criminal is equally true for the saint: The mystic, St. Thérèse Martin, has said that she began to accept the love of Christ and His cross at the age of three.[5]

I do not argue the Law of Predestination here. I am not saying that each human is a puppet programmed for a fate that is determined by the unavoidable self-recognition of his "true face." A puppet is a machine moving by the application of external forces. Not so a human being, who moves by immanent actions within a self-world of abundant choices. This side of total madness, he retains the power to resist capture by his own self-productions, even those which seem to attract him primordially. For humans are not attracted even to their most compelling ideas like stones or planets across a gravitational field. If there is recognition by a subject of some idea, there is still freedom to deny that recognition, to refuse to submit to it. The reason for this is that ideas do not appear without the willed complicity of the subject. The puppet can only capture the puppetmaster, if the latter colludes in it. He wills his own reduction to the machine level of the puppet, freely permits his own capture by a creature of his own devising:

> hide, poor dishonoured mind
> who thought yourself so wise;
> and much could understand
> concerning no and yes:
> if they've become the same
> it's time you unbecame.[6]

Here the poet tells us a number of truths. (1) That wisdom is not necessarily what the mind thinks it is; (2) that acceptance of a fate proposed by one's mind which common sense and the intellect forbids, that yes and no (good and evil) are metaphysical equals, is mistaken, and (3) that what the subject gave existence to in his mind should now be denied existence. Which is for the person to tell his erroneous mental fictions, "It's time you unbecame."

The mind is not the whole reality of the person, even if the mind lays claim to it by thinking such a grand idea. Is it possible that any person even for one moment would tolerate his own idea posing as himself? Yes. Furthermore, when there has been too much toleration of such kind, madness sets in.

It must be asked why a person permits the usurpation of himself — for that is what it is — and the installation of a self-produced fictional scenario in his place. It is because of the susceptibility of the person mixed with the expectation of pleasure that the internal "theater" of his mind affords him. This pleasure is twofold. First, it provides an escape from the blunt impact of the extra-mental world and second, it delivers with very little effort a world much nearer —at least at first — to the heart's desire. It is the old, powerful, human "conspiracy," which knows no frontiers of time or geography:

Ah Love! could you and I with Him conspire
To grasp this Sorry Scheme of Things entire,
Would not we shatter it to bits —
and then
Remould it nearer to the Heart's Desire![7]

Chapter 2
THE HABIT
OF WOUNDING
YOURSELF

My mind is no longer my friend.
It won't leave me alone.

— Lines from a poem written by a
young American college student who
then burned himself to death,
February 19, 1970.

There is only one way that your mind can turn on you and become your enemy. This is if you give reality to such a mind by a personal, internal act. Where else can your mind come from but you? It is, after all, *your* mind, is it not? Just as no one can move your finger from "inside" but you, so no one else can think with your mind. That is one of the great and central facts of your human existence, the basis of your autonomy and essential freedom.

What must be said then about those who report that their "mind is no longer my friend; it won't leave me alone"? Simply this: Such persons are mistaken; and sometimes suicide is the price they pay for making such a mistake. The mistake made by the suicide (who may be defined as one in fatal flight from a situation perceived as unbearable), was in supposing that his perception was not entirely self-produced. In one sense it is an easy mistake to make and can be crudely compared to what I will call "The Fallacy of the Light in the Refrigerator," a light supposed to be always on because, whenever one looks inside to check, it is.

If you look into your mind[1] and find there contents which are alarming, upsetting, disturbing, etc., this is not proof that such contents are there in some way independent of your own action (which is the mental equivalent of the action of opening the refrigerator door.) In fact no thoughts, good or bad, are in your mind until and unless you give reality to them *right now* by thinking them. It is you who generates your own thoughts, you who gives them the only reality they have or possibly can have.

Let us now extend the analogy of The Light in the Refrigerator. Suppose that your happiness is directly connected with the refrigerator bulb so that whenever you think it is lit, you experience mental torment. Suppose further that the torment will end only when you are sure that the light is out. Quite naturally you wish to end your torment, and so you constantly pull the door open to check on the state of the bulb. Each time you are disappointed. The irony is that it is your own action which is the cause of your torment: You need to know the connection between the light and opening the door.

Your mind and its thoughts can be compared — imperfectly to be sure — to the self-activated light. It is you, the conscious person, who initiates the activity called thinking (in effect giving reality to your mind) and who, as a consequence, generates thoughts. Accordingly, an awareness of the connection between your action and that result is critical: Until you know this truth, you cannot escape being a victim of your own activity, of wounding yourself unintentionally.

Self-wounding is a very widespread human activity. Its most extreme form is suicide, whether of the sudden or slow variety. Behind every act of suicide is the experience of mental pain, pain which prompts flight from it. Such flight is as natural as the reflex recoil of the hand from a hot stove. Such mental pain is self-produced pain and the suicide perceives this, however dimly. His act says: "I can escape the pain by escaping myself." This is like putting out the pain-causing light by attacking the refrigerator, clearly an excessive act.

One assumption can be safely made about self-wounding. It is a blunder, an error in the perception of its necessity: It is *always* better not to wound yourself.

A puzzle immediately arises about its occurrence. One is forced to conclude that there is something fundamentally indeliberate about it; humans do it, but not with knowledgeable choice. It is something they fall into against their real desires and best interests and then keep at through inertia or habit. But this can mean only one thing: Where self-wounding has become established as a fact of life, the sufferer has lost control of his life, more pointedly, of the management of his consciousness. Let us see why this must be true.

Let us go once again to our metaphor. It is true that the sufferer not only opens the refrigerator door but is aware of doing it. His is a free and fully deliberate action in the sense that nothing is *forcing* him to open the door. He is in flight from the torment that the illuminated bulb is causing him and, given his belief, his eagerness to relieve his pain is understandable. (Our hypothesis was that his torment continued just as long as he *believed* the bulb was still burning.) His repeated openings of the door are intended to accomplish something good for him. *Intended.* His action is not aimless or undirected. It is intended, chosen and deliberate. He does so with knowledge of what he is doing — opening the door in an effort to relieve his pain. Unfortunately he does not know the connection between his action and the pain in the first place. If he did, he would choose to leave the door closed. He is making a mistake *whose only cure is knowledge of the connection between his torment and his own activity.* It is good for a person to be free. Yet it must also be said that if the exercise of freedom turns the person into a victim, involves him unwittingly in a deadly process of self-wounding, such freedom is hardly worth celebrating. What does freedom profit you if you end up fleeing the effects of it into suicide or madness?

It is not freedom as some abstract exercise which benefits anyone, but freedom guided by knowledge of the way things really are.

The basic truth about your mind and its accompanying thoughts is that they come to be only by your own mental activity. Neither your mind nor your thoughts exist *unless and until you bring them into existence by an exercise of your intellect.* In other words you must literally think your mind and its thoughts into existence. This does not mean that any great conscious effort is involved. Rather the effort is frequently so slight as to go unnoticed, tempting the thinker to suppose that his thoughts are "happening" to him. And from such supposing comes the view that what happens to him cannot be his own doing, that he has no say or control over his own mental events: if he is "lucky," they are cheering and constructive; if "unlucky," they are dark, tormenting, destroying.

Human freedom is real. It lives and operates in the secret places of consciousness, where each human chooses, however unperceived, to bring into existence the events of his mental universe, events which, once real, have their corresponding effect upon him. It comes down ultimately to this: If you choose to give existence to a horror movie in your consciousness, you will experience horror. You are then not just the victim. You are also the agent of the victimization.

Yet to say your freedom is real is too abstract, too unconditioned. You must *know* you are free, precisely why and in exactly what way. You must be in possession of certain truths about reality and your involvement with it as a condition of being able to exercise your freedom. Here again, only the truth can make you free.

Notice that in all this discussion the word "you" occurs: *you* are the victim, the agent, the locus of mental and other events, the one whom the truth will liberate. *You* are the one to whom every use of the word *your*, as in *your* intellect, *your* mind, *your* thoughts, *your* will, *your* body, (including *your*self) is referred, and, without you as a ground, these terms would have no meaning or reality.

It is *you*, rather than any of your parts, powers, operations, which is the bearer of your freedom, the source from which your consciousness arises and flows as a dynamic river to your intellect, your mind, your body. You are in charge of yourself for the reason that you are yourself by a primary and simple given of nature. There is nobody or nothing haunting, hounding or tormenting yourself but *you*. Whatever is happening in your internal theater is *your* doing, the result of *your* exercise of *your* personal freedom. What makes more sense than for *you* to use *your* freedom in ways that conduce to an enlightened consciousness, a knowing intelligence, a mind undisturbed by troubling thoughts, a healthy and vital body? And what is more nonsensical than complaints by the free contriver of his own torment?

It must now be asked: Why would you deliberately torment yourself? What possible gain can there be for you to do so? What discernible motivation? Clearly there can be no gain which is not vastly and immediately outweighed by losses. And yet self-wounding is a widespread human phenomenon: Suicide in its quick and slow forms is a commonplace of everyday life. What is the explanation for this extraordinary paradox?

It is the drama of human freedom. Each human freely manages his own consciousness (who else is there to do it?), but many are then reduced to fleeing the mental torments which they freely produce.

Here you may disagree. Many people, you say, are in flight from horrors which real events press on their consciousness, from disease, debts, dangers, death of loved ones.

Yet surely for each human who is subject to the immediate and cruel shock of some personal tragedy, there are thousands who are tormented by the fear or expectation of it. In effect, they are tormented by what they have imagined. No real event has battered its way into their consciousness: What haunts them is spawned within their minds and arises as a result of the free (though often only dimly conscious) exercise of their intellects.

For those who suffer the intrusive shock of some real tragedy in their lives, the immediate pain of grief and of loss is undoubtedly involuntary. There is an instinctive and understandable flight from pain into disbelief, hysteria, unconsciousness. Time here is the victims' ally, provided the "healing tissue of forgetfulness" which grows naturally over the psychic wound is not continually torn away by repeated voluntary acts of morbid remembrance or by unacceptance of the reality, that is to say, when the involuntary wound is not compounded by self-wounding.

Chapter 3
TROUBLES

Whatever flames upon the night
Man's own resinous heart has fed.

— William Butler Yeats

One hears a lot of what passes for basic strategy for troubles. Thus, one person will be heard to say, "Basically, I've got a money problem," when what he really has is an incurable disease. For he is sure that just as John D. Rockefeller lived to be ninety-seven because he could buy the best in medical treatment, so could *he* be cured. . . with enough money.

Again, one hears a man on his way to prison for embezzlement say, "If I had the right lawyer, this would never have happened. The right lawyer would have kept me out of trouble," presumably from the day of birth.

Or, more commonly, troubles are said to be basically due to "bad luck." Thus untold multitudes try to change their luck by divining the right day or moment for everything from the astrology charts.

Basic. The word pops up in human speech so much these days that its misuse was inevitable. We know what basic black is: the absorption of all color; or basic white: the reflection of all color. But what is the meaning of *basic* yellow? or *basic* brown?

If our remedies are only as good as the lawyers, psychiatrists, counselors and astrologers at our disposal, how basic is that? If the way out of our troubles is on the frail vehicles of money, human integrity, or luck, where is the basis of any successful journey?

A trouble exists or it doesn't. If it doesn't, there is no problem; if it does, the task is to contrive to make it non-existent. That is what I mean by being basic: *that the trouble exists.* And if that is not your understanding of the true meaning of the word *basic* in this context, you should read no further; this book is not for you.

I have said troubles are all alike, even while they differ. What I meant was simply this: troubles are alike in that they are real, they exist. And here I am not distinguishing troubles that your physician says are "only in your mind," so-called psychosomatic ailments, from "real" ones, that is to say, genuinely physical ones. No, if a trouble is real to you, it's real, *period.*

Here one is reminded of the story of the woman with the ailing husband, advised by a friend to ignore his complaints because, like the friend's husband's ailments, they were entirely mental. "Don't pay any attention to him; he only thinks he's sick," said the friend, such advice being given a number of times over a period of several months. Then one day the friend again inquired about the husband's health. "He thinks he's dead," answered the woman. And he was.

The point I wish to make with the story is that while the man's death proved that he had an ailment, a non-death wouldn't prove he didn't. If the sufferer thinks he's sick, that, trouble-wise, is sufficient to warrant our attention. Sickness and trouble do not necessarily go together. People die everyday who didn't know they were sick. (Did they die from being sick or from being mortal?). Untroubled by concern for their health, they naturally took no medical action, something which troubles their survivors, even as they envy that "marvelous way of dying."

Trouble. Who needs it? Particularly when it sets up independent housekeeping, so to speak, in your consciousness, becoming the star, non-paying boarder.

A trouble "pays its way" by prompting an appropriate course of action. The appropriate course of action then eliminates the trouble. Thus the man troubled by failing eyesight goes to the ophthalmologist, who effects a cure. The trouble then disappears. Such trouble is productive, useful, even a blessing.

It is when trouble does not pay its way, but rather charges the host for the dubious pleasure of its company that it deserves immediate eviction.

There are only two general states of reality of which ordinary human consciousness is aware. This is made clear if we take the case of a patient ill with heart disease. The disease is an objective fact, registering not only on the electrocardiograph, but also in the physical appearance and condition of the patient. It is a state of real being. There is another state of being, created by the patient's consciousness, which although not directly subject to objective proofs of its existence, is real, too. This state is the patient's awareness of his illness. These two states of reality, represented by a physical illness and the patient's (or anyone else's) awareness of that illness, are the two basic classes of reality, technically called objective and subjective states of being, respectively.

The objective state, the illness, is "out there." It is not an idea or a dream; it cannot be wished away or ignored into non-existence. Awake or asleep it is a reality. It has physical manifestations, a definite locus in space (it may be confined to a distinct part of the body or be body-wide), and a definite time-fix — now (with some history or past and some prognosis or future as curable or terminal). The trouble, as I define trouble, is not in the objective reality, but in the subjective state.

A form of friendly advice often given to the troubled is expressed as follows: Try not to think about your troubles. Here is a case where the addition of one word tends to render such advice virtually useless, like giving a lock combination with one wrong number. That word is "about," which suggests that one's trouble is "out there," like the tumor.[1] If it were, clearly not thinking about the trouble would be as unavailing as not thinking about the tumor, for the tumor *is* really "out there," no matter what one's thoughts on the subject at that moment. And here I say "at the moment" deliberately, because there seems to be some recognition by medical scientists that a basic change of consciousness maintained *over some length of time* can upset the most definitive prognosis of a disease.

The subjective state is the *immediate* cause of the problem. This becomes clear when one perceives that it is the existence of the trouble in the consciousness that is the basic fact about it. No doubt the disease itself occasions the event in the consciousness but, and this cannot be overemphasized, it is the consciousness itself which generates the trouble, not the disease. Here an analogy may help. A house is burning to the ground. What is the cause of it? Why, the fire, of course, How about the pyromaniac who applied the match, having first scattered the gasoline? Is he not the cause of the destruction of the house? Legally and morally, yes; physically no. The reality of the fire on combustible material produced the result: only fire burns. Furthermore the fire was in the same space coordinate as the house; the man had left the scene and by the time the fire was really going, he was miles away.

The analogy does not fit the case perfectly — no analogy ever does. Yet it does serve to illumine the actual nature and cause of trouble. The fire must be actually burning on the scene to do the damage; should it at any moment go out, the destruction ends. It is the same with trouble. Trouble is generated by an act of human consciousness present at the scene of the sufferer. Like the fire, it has its effect (trouble/ destruction) *only during those actual moments of the generating consciousness.* Just as the pyromaniac's action would have had no effect on the house if the fire did not burn, so the disease can have no power to generate trouble if the patient's consciousness does not generate it. The brain of the pyromaniac generates pyromania naturally, not fire; and the tumor in the patient generates physical debilitation, not trouble. This is proved conclusively by the fact that people can be troubled by imaginary diseases.

Thus the friendly advice to the suffering patient should not be to stop thinking *about* his troubles, but to stop *thinking* them, that is, to stop generating them. But the success of this modified advice depends upon the sufferer's understanding what the words say — that the sufferer's troubles are self-generated, that is, they arise within the consciousness by a specific act of that consciousness. Which means, basically, that trouble is willed into existence, however unperceived that fact may be.

Thus the strategy of dealing directly with your troubles at the very fountainhead of their being is, and must be, the prime strategy because it bears on the reality of trouble; also, it is a strategy "for all seasons," that is to say, for all troubles of whatever kind. For while the kind is determined by the particular setting which occasions it — money troubles, family troubles, health troubles — each is caused by a specific act of consciousness in real time (a now) and can have no reality apart from such an act.

And it is when this truth about your troubles is understood and practiced with skill that you are able to escape the really disabling effects of adverse circumstances: They can no longer trouble you, because *you know how not to trouble yourself.*

At the same time, you will retain the power to let trouble educate you and direct you into appropriate action. Your aim will not be a simple-minded, trouble-free existence, but rather a life which is as trouble-free as common sense lets it be.

Chapter 4
STAYING SANE

Is it the flag that moves? Is it the wind?
Neither: it is your mind.

— Hui-Neng, The Sixth Ch'an Patriarch

If you were given the choice of being executed immediately or rendered unconscious for the rest of your natural life and then put to death, wouldn't you just as soon die immediately? Understandably you have no interest in life which you would share with the cauliflower, that is to say, in mere bodily existence.

No, consciousness is central in your life, all important, valued and loved beyond all other aspects of yourself. It enjoys a gloriously unique status. Let us now examine this fact about consciousness closely.

A common error is to identify consciousness with thinking. The error is understandable because thinking gives a special edge or focus to awareness, lighting it up, as it were, in a special way. Yet to confuse one with the other is to mistake the part for the whole, which is like pushing a literary device called the synecdoche beyond its proper use. The poet may speak of the "sail" on the water, but everyone knows it is a ship. Thus a few thoughts that one is producing in a particular unit of time are not the whole of your consciousness, nor, indeed, the way you "are" during that time and to think so is erroneous.

Thoughts have a distinctly different kind of reality from consciousness (and of course from the brain as well). Even if thoughts are no more than a "phosphorescent scum" on the brain, as the materialist psychologist might say, they are unique realities, products of a unique activity called thinking.

For this and several other reasons, thinking should not be confused with consciousness, the former being a particular state of awareness within a much larger field of awareness. Thinking is limited consciousness and therefore can serve only limited purposes. It is precisely to escape such limitations resulting from thought that meditational practices such as Zen exist. For until the mind is "stilled," true knowledge, the wider consciousness, held at bay by thought, cannot be realized. Thus Hugh L'Anson Fausset tells us:

> All meditation is based in the conviction that we have only to acknowledge and assent to the Reality from which we have never in essence been separated to awake from the long illusion of the ego. In doing so we shall cease to think about Truth and realize Truth itself. The transition from thinking to knowing, the fulfillment of Mindfulness in "No-Mind" will have been effected.[1]

We use the word "realize" in common speech without attention to the full meaning of that word, to the distinctions entailed in it. To realize that an object in the distance, on approaching, is a man, is to put that object into a category, to produce a thought about that object, and to give it a realization in your mind. No doubt the object in question is a man, but he is not a thought and therefore in no way is his reality adequately captured in the thought. When one consults one's thinking for the "answer" to what the object is, the answer is immediately given: It is a man. At this point, the perceptive person will become aware of a gap, which he will close if he can: He will try to realize the man more adequately than he did by conceptualizing him. Instinctively, he tries to accomplish this through improving his thinking, encouraged by his early success in accurately classifying his object. And so begins the enterprise of thinking until an elaborate system is constructed. He finds many works in the libraries to speed him on his way by furnishing him with rules of logic and a full-blown vocabulary. It is a labor, but if he has even a little aptitude for it, as many humans have, it can be very enjoyable. If he is gifted he can call himself a philosopher, one whose consuming interest is Man. Yet if he is a true philosopher, he will soon understand that he has done little to close the gap between that mysterious figure out there with arms and legs and a human face, and a realization of him in his thought. And the same problem will hold true for self-realization, or the passage from thinking of yourself in categories to knowing yourself in a direct and immediate way.

Yet, paradoxically, for all the limitedness of thought compared to the large field of consciousness itself, it is through thinking that the human person most commonly becomes aware of consciousness. And if this seems a little like the tail wagging the dog, in many instances the analogy is apt. Tragically so. For unless restrained, thought has a way of gripping or absorbing consciousness to the point of possessing it, as it were, totally. In such cases the whole consciousness, indeed the whole person, *becomes* his thought. That is why we can speak of a person caught up in thought, deep in thought, and — not a rare phenomenon — obsessed by thought, the latter creating a bond so tight and so complete that the autonomy of the person is lost and his condition pathological.

You may ask: Is there some rule or principle by which insanity may be characterized as distinguished from the sane or normal state of human consciousness?

Speaking generally, this much at least can be said (paraphrasing the familiar Arabian proverb): He who thinks and is able to be aware reflectively that he thinks, is sane, while he who thinks and is reflectively incapable of such awareness is insane.

Again speaking generally, all those of the first class still enjoy their own autonomy, indicated by a consciousness which, as it were, keeps the thinking process in view and thereby domesticates and confines it. Thought has not eaten up the consciousness and is playing an essentially useful role to the consciousness and the whole person. Thinking here has a purely instrumental function.

The second class covered by the proverb is insane, more or less severely depending upon the degree of absorption of the consciousness and the person by thought. In the extreme case, there is no operating space, as it were, for the consciousness — that is, space not occupied by the mind thinking its thoughts, generating those self-produced, self-willed fields of force which require adherence to its imperatives.[2]

If there is one mark common to the vast population of insane people in the world, it is their absorption by thought, and if there are degrees of insanity among the insane, as there clearly are, the degree is in proportion to the absorption by thought. The totally insane have "gone over" to thought; it is their food and drink, their mother and father, their whole universe. The connection to the objective world has been severed, and helping them clinically is perhaps as hard as entering a person's dream and there ministering to him. They are hopeless cases, and whether it is because of some persistent action of will on the part of the totally insane who choose to remain in that state (Laing and Maslow and others are on record as viewing insanity as a rational adjustment, the best under the circumstances, by the subject to his personal predicament) or whether they are just helpless victims, need not detain us here. It is enough to know the role that thought plays in the genesis of insanity as a means of preventing the condition in your own case.

This much at least, however, must be said: Even the totally insane are doing it to themselves, and when we speak of them as helpless victims, we do not for a moment suppose that they are not producing the mental states that hold them in an iron grip. Still, they are not to be blamed for doing what they do to themselves. Their thought-obsessed state has so overrun the willed actions which produce the state that there is no longer any consciousness of what is being willed. There is total mindfulness, a co-opting by thought so complete that, effectively speaking, the autonomy of the person has vanished.

If this is clearly understood, a long step has been taken by the currently sane who wish to remain so; for here again, knowledge is power, in this case the very power to confine thought to its indispensable role as servant of the consciousness, thereby preventing it from becoming its master.

An alarming number of people become insane, so complacency on the part of anyone about this widespread condition is misguided, if not foolish. If our theory is correct, insanity is no respecter of persons, literally not of anyone, however insulated against it he may think he is by heredity, conditioning, or whatever. For as a "thinking animal," man is an active producer of that petard on which, unless wary, he can he hoist. He must thus take into full account the fact that he is a thinking animal and all that this implies, as it bears on his mental health.

If he is to remain a *sane* thinking animal, he cannot plunge blithely ahead with ungoverned thinking, supremely confident that he is doing something natural or, even worse, remain oblivious to the dangers of his activity. Thoughts are potent stuff and insouciance in the handling of dynamite is perhaps not as dangerous. The phrase, "We are what we think," affirms this danger. For consider: If indeed we are what we think, then, if we care what we are, the most careful guarding of our thoughts urgently recommends itself. But if the phrase is modified to read, "We are in danger of becoming what we think *when we think*," then a certain new element of control with respect to thought enters the picture. Now instead of selecting only the safer or choicer thoughts for our company, in the way in which we would join only the better clubs, we choose whether to belong to any club at all continuously, or to join or resign at will as it suits us.

The problem for the sane is simply this: How to think and still not be captured by thought. One likes to believe that had the insane been forewarned about the dangers of ungoverned thought, like a man approaching quicksand who sees the warning sign in time and changes his direction, they might have been able to halt a drift toward that unhappy state. Clearly this could only have been accomplished while autonomy was still intact, when the person was still able to will his inner orientation away from the "planet" of his thoughts, with its strong magnetic pull on his consciousness. For thoughts and their systems generate what might be called fields of force whose strength is a function of their intensity of generation and their continuity. Here, of course, we are speaking only analogously and making a comparison to physical being; but if the analogy is not stretched too far, it can help us to visualize the dynamics of the problem.

Up to now you may have supposed that the insanity that is being discussed is what is called the socially aberrant, certifiable kind associated in most people's minds with tranquilizing drugs, straitjackets, asylums with attending staffs, and the insane only those luckless souls driven blindly to inflict harm on themselves or on others. A man who would leap from a bridge to his death, a woman who would drown her own children, are adjudged insane. There is no quarrel with this judgment except that it is too restricted. When Adolf Hitler began ordering millions of humans to their deaths, somehow his certification as insane did not arise in common consciousness, as it instantly does for the bridge-leaper. Hitler wasn't blindly committing his murders but knew precisely what he was doing and willed it freely and dispassionately? The theory of blindness or lack of it in adjudging insanity clearly has flaws, both because of its arbitrariness and its fuzziness. When a man is blind and, because of it, walks off a cliff, that is a clear causal connection; but what is "blindness" when analogized to the question of madness?

Let us propose a new criterion for insanity, a criterion which escapes both arbitrariness and fuzziness: Let the subject be examined for the degree of his capture by thought and adjudged sane or not on that test.

Using this criterion, both the bridge-jumper and Adolf Hitler were insane, both totally captured by thought and only different in the target against which their respective madnesses were directed. Both launched an all-out attack on perceived "enemies": the suicide, himself; Hitler, the Jews. Both acted blindly, their consciousness totally eclipsed by thought, their human freedom nullified by its hypnotizing action.

To an alarming degree, each person is incipiently a bridge-jumper or a mad dictator, and it is false to suppose that the insane are different breeds from the rest of us, harboring organic tendencies or weaknesses leading to a madness of which we need have no real fear. The truth is that each of us is separated from madness by a razor's edge, by that slender and terribly frail bit of knowledge which a provident nature grants us, a gift which is nonetheless sufficient to keep us sane our whole life through. This is (going back to the proverb) to think and to know that we think.

Chapter 5
ON BEING
AWARE
OF YOURSELF

Babylon in all its desolation is a sight not so awful as that of the human mind in ruins.

— Scrope Davies

There are many uncertainties about the mentally ill but at least one safe generality can be made. It is this: The psychotic doesn't have self-awareness. Or perhaps it might be safer to say that during moments, if any, when a psychotic is self-aware, he is not psychotic.

The psychotic is someone captured so thoroughly by his own mental self-productions, that he has lost the power to will an independent act of real self-awareness. He thinks and does not know he is thinking, all with abundant energy and extravagant productivity. The psychotic hears, sees, smells, tastes, feels in his own peculiar way; which is to say, he is in touch only — or at least dominantly — with his own self-produced universe.

The psychotic lives in a veritable redoubt, insulated from intrusion from the outside (whether by another person or even by the "outside" self of the psychotic), and it takes a highly concentrated attack on this redoubt to breach it. This is precisely what shock therapy — appropriately named — accomplishes: it literally breaks into the psychotic's mental stronghold by force, e.g., by a blow of electricity or insulin, and swings the balance of autonomy back to the larger consciousness. The psychotic is now no longer psychotic: he has been summoned back to the world outside of his thought and rendered able — at least for awhile — to be self-aware. He is not by that fact cured, however, as clinical experience with the psychotic patient shows with disappointing regularity; old habits of thinking remain powerfully latent in the nerve pathways and are there to be fallen into again, unless steps are taken at once to prevent the pull of the familiar on the consciousness.

The therapist can play a crucial role in preventing this, if he directs his patient realistically, with a knowledge of the way consciousness and reality *really are*. The therapist needs to be a metaphysician. He must know what is real and how to find it. He must be able to help his psychotic patient regain his own autonomy, his power to become self-aware. Should the therapist fail in this primary task, the psychotic is doomed to slip back and be re-captured by his own self-productions.

The psychotic is socially dysfunctional. It is primarily by this "sign" that we know him. Yet this is not why he is psychotic: it is because there is no operational freedom in him. One of the chief things that being mentally healthy means is that one is free. This freedom presupposes knowledge. The psychotic may seem to possess knowledge but it is mere information as held by a computer, and therefore not knowledge at all. The psychotic may give many reassuring signs that he under-stands, that he knows, yet these signs are blind. They imply no deeper realization within the consciousness of the subject: The knowledge is a kind of magnetic impression on the "tape" of consciousness with no registration on the consciousness itself. The knowledge is not alive. This is because the psychotic is not alive in the operational sense, even though, again, all the biological, medical, and even psychological indices may be flashing.

The psychotic is, as psychiatric jargon puts it, compulsive. This means that he is continually being hurtled along by the productions within his own consciousness to unsocial acts, acts which may show great ingenuity and creativity. He faithfully acts out the self-produced scenario taking place within his mind, a mind which, before long, becomes exper-ienced in luxuriant and inventive theater but which con-stitutes a "closed loop" — what the psychotic experiences, he also is producing.

In fact, *all* human minds are "closed loops," which is simply to say that the mind, taken as mind, feeds on its own productions. It is autonomous. It doesn't need anything outside of itself, except indirectly. The mind thinks its own internally produced material, its thoughts. How then is the psychotic mind different, as it clearly is? It is different in the crucial respect that the mind of the psychotic has "captured" the whole conscious self-hood of the subject, that is to say, reduced it to one of its own fictions. When this takes place, the freedom of the subject disappears down the "rabbit-hole" of mind.

The word mind is frequently used as a synonym for intellect or even for consciousness. This is false. The mind is neither the intellect nor the consciousness, as one's internal experience will quickly show. To think is not to know or even to be aware. To think is for the self to perform an act of mind within consciousness. Only the mind can set up an entire universe of its own over against the world of objective reality. This is an awesome power, and it will be well for us to spend some time considering this universe of mind.

To begin with, every universe is real. If it weren't, it would correspond to nothing. But what is nothing? If we examine the word nothing, we face two more basic words, "no" and "thing." Thus, literally, "nothing" means the absence, the removal, of some "thing": Now you see it (a tree, a bird, a man); now you don't. Cut the tree down, scare the bird away, dismiss the man and what is left, so to speak, is the "nothing" of the thing that previously was there.[1]

It is the same with thoughts. Think, for example, of a cobra, then switch to the thought of an ostrich, and the first thought is gone — it is reduced to nothing. We thus have our proof that both the universe of *things*, like planets or people, and of *thoughts*, like the thought of a planet, of people, are real, i.e., more than nothing. For all the remarkable differences between the *lion* in the field and the *thought* of the lion in the field, they both *belong to the real universe*.[2]

The mind then is real. Yet the mind is still not a thing, like the intellect. The mind is a creation of the intellect reflecting upon its contents. The mind is the intellect in a closed loop operation, where the reference is inward instead of to the world of things outside. Let me be concrete. The knower, using his intellect, grasps what John Jones is, a human being. Now suppose the knower becomes interested in the concept itself, as opposed to Jones the man. He then uses his intellect to consider human being directly, transforming that concept into an idea and changing his intellect into his mind. He is now no longer knowing the outside world but "minding" the contents of his own consciousness.

The mind is now thinking, producing thoughts. This thinking is a real activity and, since it is, the products of such a real activity are real. Our experience confirms this. Whatever you produce in your mind is really there, to exhilarate or to depress you, to enlight or to darken you, to do this to you or that, depending upon what you produce in your mind. The law of mental causality is as rigid and predictable as the law of physical causality, e.g., of falling bodies. Thinking is serious business; and since it is, it needs to be done carefully and well.

What does this mean, to think carefully and well? It means in the primary sense to be aware that thinking is taking place. Yet this at once introduces a special problem. One cannot think and be aware of it simultaneously. Experience confirms this. If there is any doubt, try right now to imagine an elephant and at the same time be aware that you are imagining. One activity excludes the other. All of us have had the rather remarkable experience of doing something, such as driving a car a long distance, without being aware that we are doing it. We were on "automatic pilot," doing something which has been established as a habit, and all while we were unaware of it. And what were we primarily engaged in during that interval? In thinking, in producing mental beings within the closed loop of the mind, beings which held us fascinated with a rich, self-produced mental scenario.

Such productions are natural. True. And it is equally true to say that the obsessive-compulsive productions of the psychotic are "natural," as well, in that (a) "Nature" produces every-thing, and (b) it is "natural" for a psychotic to have a psychotic mental life. So that the test of any reality cannot simply be in terms of *What is Natural*. Nor, for that matter, simply in terms of *What is Normal*. The psychotic could be called normal given the set of mental states he is internally producing. Indeed, he regards himself as normal (and everybody else crazy). Norms are always set by *individuals* even when they act as a group. Of course, the norm of the psychotic seldom prevails; his bizarre conduct soon sees him constrained. Yet not always, and we need look no farther than Adolf Hitler or Josef Stalin for confirmation of this.

The productions of the psychotic are "unnatural" or "abnor-mal" because they are subject to no internal challenges to their being. The mind has effectively displaced the person and his intellect, dethroned both of them.

The self is the person's connection with the objectively real universe. Among the healthy person's most precious and urgent powers is awareness of that self — a power he uses frequently to govern his mind. The psychotic has, for a variety of reasons, lost the use of that power. It is the essential work of the therapist, as we said earlier, to show his patient how to find that power and then to keep it. Sadly, for many psychotics, it is already too late, even with the best of help. This should serve as a warning to everyone this side of psychosis who cherishes his sanity and is determined to do all in his power to preserve it.

You cannot think and at the same time know that you are thinking. One state precludes the other. In that crucial respect, the mind of the maniac and of the sane person are identical. Yet they differ critically — they differ in that the maniac has lost the power to "recover" from his thought, which means to be aware again of the extra-mental world, including the awareness of himself.

Once that awareness of the real world outside of thought is lost, once thought has "eaten up" the whole of consciousness, we can say the person has become ideologized, which is another way of saying that he is insane. And his social conduct bears unmistakable clinical evidence of that fact in his bizarre, anti-social behavior.

Chapter 6
THE UNENCUMBERED NOW

Anyone who goes to a psychiatrist should have his head examined.

— Samuel Goldwyn

According to current psychoanalytic theory one of the worst things you can do is to repress a bad experience. Not only do you not get rid of the dirt you sweep under the rug but, according to the theory, the dirt has a way of collecting itself into a critical mass which then starts ticking away in your consciousness, ultimately to explode with devastating results to your psyche. If you are lucky, the damage is limited to a waste of your vital resources in order to maintain the repression. What you need to do is to face the experience honestly and courageously, the theory goes, and, with the help of your analyst, drain it of its power to poison and traumatize you.

I have a major quarrel with this theory.

In point of fact, there is no way that any experience can be repressed, if by experience we mean some concrete social deed done in real time. The person who commits some deed, horrible or otherwise, moves immediately away from it in time. He had an experience, the experience passed. What is in past time simply no longer is. Therefore, there is no way he can repress the *experience* and it is pure nonsense to claim otherwise.

If we must talk about repression then, let us talk about the repression of the only reality possible under the circumstances, and that is the reality of the *remembered* event. Yet, clearly, remembered events are not repressible until and unless they appear in the consciousness. Appear? To speak of memories of past events "appearing" in consciousness is to overlook the fact that most remembrances are the result of *willed* acts by the subject, however unperceived this may be. Even those remembrances which the subject does not directly will, those which arise, as it were, spontaneously, need the subject's willed activity to prolong them in consciousness.[1]

That is why a theory of the *production* of recollections makes sense where repression theory makes little or none. You cannot repress what you do not produce: it is as simple as that. But let us go at once to a concrete illustration.

The memory of some unspeakable deed is making a living hell out of your consciousness. You did it years ago, have regretted it a million times, have in a sense paid for it with mountains of grief and remorse, but it still tortures you. You would be done with it, but it will not be done with you. You dream of escape from it, but your waking moments are filled with despair over that happy possibility. The thought of its pursuit of you for the rest of your life is frequently more than you can bear. Opposed as you are to suicide, you find that temptation present in your consciousness more than you would like to admit, and this is an added burden to you, even as the thought of its relief tantalizes you.

If reality is so structured that your bad experience is carried along through time with its full cargo of reality, you are in as much trouble as you may think. You are like some weakened Hercules carrying a crushing weight on your shoulders with the ratio disfavoring you as the years pile up.

Fortunately for you and for the rest of us, too, reality is not so constituted. Experiences that happen *had* their reality.[2] If you think you *have* a problem when in fact you merely *had* one, you have assumed a burden imposed not by time but by yourself and are mistakenly refusing the gift of the unencumbered now that time continuously offers.

The unencumbered now. Blessedly the now arrives for everyone totally free of past events whether large or small, crucial or trivial. The now is simply and purely now and has a nature completely its own, which is to say utterly different from the past or the future. Not only are there no past or future elements in it, there are not even any hints or rumbles or contaminations from other times. The now is now precisely because the past has been totally and unrecoverably shed, the future totally and unequivocally unborn. The now is a beginning again for all beings which enter its chaste, holy, and mysterious precinct. There is perhaps no better way to speak about this mystery than to say that the now *is* and any drift in thought or speech toward the *was* of the past or the *will be* of the future as regards the now is the falsest of errors. What is cannot be that which is not, which is the essential meaning of what was and what will be.

The man who walks away from a severed hand and makes up his mind to accept what happened and to be with what now is, is manifesting the kind of respect for time and reality which both require. Insanity is spawned by the habit of resisting what is, by attempts to confer now-status on what was or will be. No human will, however determined or steady in its intentions, can stand against the "will" of reality to be what it really is. Some fortunate humans learn this quickly, some more slowly, some (it would seem) never, and if psychoanalytic theory would have a project worthy of its fervor and energies, what better one than to sensitize its stricken charges to the way the world is?

Given these simple truths about time and reality, what possible basis in reality can there be for a theory which proposes that there is somehow something carried into the now from the past which is repressible apart from the subject's own specific willed mental activity? Let the repression theorists show, if they can, what this independent reality is, independent in the sense that the subject comes upon it much as he might a tree in his garden.

The first and real problem then is the one dealing with the production of the material in the consciousness rather than with repressing that which is already produced. *One cannot repress what one does not create.* It is as simple as that.

Does the subject suffer from the reality of what he did? And here the word "reality" is apt and true, for there is no suffering over nothing. It is immensely helpful to learn about the true nature of such traumas as remorse for what one did, losses one has suffered, griefs one has experienced. And the key to that reality is encapsulated in the word "has," which will tell the sufferer that his experience is *past,* that he has lived through it and survived it, that he occupies the blessed precinct of the unencumbered now, and that, if he truly wants relief, he will find it in the now, in the discovery that the now is absolutely a new, uncontaminated beginning, free of the past and unbound to any future.

Unfortunately most people drag their past around like Marley's chains; and whether or not Dickens was trying to make a metaphysical point in having the bearer of the chains a ghost, he succeeded in showing how one becomes a Scrooge. For Scrooge is the prototype of someone who continuously packs his unencumbered nows with the contents of past time, giving a form of life in his consciousness to reluctant ghosts of time gone by. For even Christmases gone by, if kept speciously alive, will encumber the present with that feature which the now will not, indeed cannot, tolerate — the slightest trace of pastness. But even Scrooge, so habituated to creating past time in his consciousness, could wake up and in a moment discover the weightlessness of the now. Once the miracle of Tiny Tim's rebirth in health broke with full force into his consciousness, and he saw the marvelous newness of the whole world, he became fired with new life, new freedom, an exhilarating sense of his grand opportunity to participate actively in the coming-to-be of a brand new world.

Chapter 7
THE
MIGHT-HAVE-BEEN
MISERIES

These poor Might-Have-Beens,
These fatuous, ineffectual Yesterdays!

— William Ernest Henley

Robert Frost once wrote a poem entitled "The Road Not Taken." It will repay us to reflect on what he says in it:

> I shall be telling this with a sigh
> Somewhere ages and ages hence:
> Two roads diverged in a wood, and I —
> I took the one less traveled by,
> And that made all the difference.[1]

The poet is predicting that he will one day be troubling himself with what can be called his "might-have-beens." It is human to do so, and Frost proved to be very human: jealous of his poetic reputation, severely critical of his loved ones and friends, often sour on life. A loveable elf in appearance, he is revealed in biographies as having a dark, brooding underside, tortured by a variety of agonies. Clearly he knew a full measure of the "Might-have-been Miseries."

The habit of envisioning how life might have gone had one taken another road, had things worked out differently in one's life, had this or that happened or not happened, occurs widely in humans. And it brings to them, just as it seems to have brought to Frost, discontent, grief, worry, regret. It afflicts those whose might-have-beens are visualized as always happier, more successful, more fulfilling than what actually happened. If there is misery in the present, it is intensified by its shadowy contrast to the sunshine of what was missed. There is no allowance made for a miserable might-have-been, for some tragedy at the end of the road not taken. The victims of the syndrome never seem to realize that any given might-have-been, so splendid when imagined, might have been a good deal worse than what occurred.

Frost tells us in the poem that he studied the scene at the fork and chose carefully:

> . . . long I stood
> And looked down one as far as I could
> To where it bent in the undergrowth.[2]

He did not flip a coin or give way to whim or impulse. No, he pondered the choices open to him and picked the one with more appeal — though regretfully — for both roads beckoned. The problem was that he could not "travel both and be one traveler." And his regret persisted: He saw enough of the road not taken to pique his interest and to charge his memory with its rich possibilities. And, though he was forced to take only one road, a part of him was split by the choice and never came together again. He always remembered the tantalizing "difference" of the other road.

The pattern lived and described by Frost so beautifully is a familiar one. We all see other roads, other possibilities than the ones we decide upon. We are not forced to pick what we do, but only to limit ourselves to it. This limitation leaves us unreconciled, grieves us in the measure that we visualize and remember the attractions of the "road not taken" — especially in the light of the hard realities of the one that was.

There can be joy in the abstract feeling of being in a position to choose; unfortunately it often does not carry over to the concrete act of choice itself, which can be wearing and even painful. Because of the risks and fatigues of exercising choice, the forsaking of all choice can also be joyful, perhaps more so than the abstract feeling of being free. In his recent book, Peter Matthiessen tells about his meeting with a crippled Lama in the high mountains of northern Nepal.

> The Lama of the Crystal Monastery appears to be a very happy man, and yet I wonder how he feels about his isolation in the silences of Tsakang, which he has not left in eight years now and, because of his legs, may never leave again. . . Indicating his twisted legs without a trace of self-pity or bitterness, as if they belonged to all of us, he casts his arms wide to the sky and the snow mountains, the high sun and dancing sheep, and cries, "Of course I am happy here! It's wonderful! *Especially* when I have no choice!"[3]

When there is absolutely no choice, there can be no might-have-beens, no road not taken. There can be no material for regret that one did not choose well, or even that one was limited only to one road to travel. This, as the Lama reported, can be wonderful.

The trouble is that, save for exceptional situations, life is alive with choices. We can delay many decisions about the road to take, but such delay is itself a decision and a choice. And whether we delay or act, we face the foreclosing, first, of all that might be and, later on, of what might-have-been, when we have acted on our choice.

Up to now we have been considering might-have-been miseries arising from the act of choosing. But how about the kind that comes without any choosing, such as the death of a loved one in an accident? In such a case the sense that it could easily have been otherwise can become a torment: *If only* he had waited for the light; *if only* she had taken another flight; *if only* the gun had not been loaded. The thought that the loved one might still be alive but for a chance coincidence of forces, that a precious spouse or child, parent, or friend was snatched away in a mindless, preventable accident gives the survivor no rest in his compulsive review of the event. The mind disbelieves; it refuses to accept the blow; it probes untiringly for the flaw in the logic that will magically restore the victim to life. Some, unable to accept the cruel unluckiness of it all, embrace madness or suicide as the only relief.

There seem to be two kinds of might-have-been miseries, one arising from choice and the other from unchosen circumstance. In the first instance we look back on the road we chose not to take and torture ourselves with how different, how beautiful, how magical it all might have been; in the second we agonize over a loss that might have been otherwise but for a cruel trick of fate. In both cases the "if only" complaint sounds in the mouth of the sufferer, echoing the mind's deep lament. It is a dirge which tells of the sufferer's troubled mind, so endlessly busy with reviewing his loss, with placing blame, with positing whys, with measuring his misery, etc.

If madness can be defined as the capture of consciousness by the mind, i.e., by a system of thoughts, manifesting the subject's reluctance and/or inability to break the captivity, then surely the person in the thick of might-have-been miseries, caught up in mental exercises which solve nothing and churn him endlessly around a fixed point of anguish, is mad. No doubt there are degrees of madness and the preoccupation with one's might-have-been admits of degree, clinically evidenced by social behavior. Shakespeare gave us a penetrating picture of the immobilization that madness caused in the case of Lady Macbeth:

> Doctor.   Not so sick, my Lord,
> As she is troubled with thick-coming fancies,
> That keep her from rest.

> Macbeth.   Cure her of that:
> Canst thou not minister to a mind diseased,
> Pluck from memory a rooted sorrow,
> Raze out the written troubles of the brain. . .[4]

As also did Yeats, telling about the bizarre speech of Crazy Jane:

> Bring me to the blasted oak
> That I, midnight upon the stroke
> (All find safety in the tomb.)
> May call down curses on his head
> Because of my dear Jack that's dead.[5]

Both women were victims of madness induced by the vision of what might-have-been: a queen, whose "thick-coming fancies" were surely of a safe and legitimate reign beside her husband-king; an Irishwoman, whose dreams were of happy conjugal life, if only her "dear Jack" had not died. The plights of these sufferers, immortalized by two poets' attentions, have dramatic force precisely because they present a widespread human tendency to succumb to the bewitching power of the miseries of the mind's imagining. But what is to be done about such miseries? Again another poet speaks:

> Misery is a good thing if misery is spread,
> One hurt at a time, so relief feels good;

> But when misery begins to bite bone,
> And the sweet marrow is my own,
> Then misery is nothing to talk about.
> Misery must be killed and thrown out.[6]

Misery must be killed and thrown out. Yes. And particularly that misery which arises from the brooding over our might-have-beens: so wasting of our modest ration of present time, so corrosive of our contentment with what actually came to pass, so useless for any improvement of our lives. How is such deep and widespread human misery as this to be "killed and thrown out"?

The answer is that the remedy for this particular misery must come from the resources of the self. It comes down to this prescription: *Since you and no one else is generating the misery, you and you alone can stop it.* Were it not that way, were it not true that the host of this misery is also the generator of it, then the self could correctly look elsewhere for relief. Yet it *is* true. One of the great evidences of natural justice is that the perpetrator of the mischief be its primary victim. And because this is generally perceived, the sufferer of such misery finds that he has soon exhausted the patience even of the most sympathetic. Weep too long over might-have-been imaginings, and you soon are weeping alone.

> Laugh, and the world laughs with you;
> Weep and you weep alone;
> For the sad old earth must borrow its mirth,
> But has trouble enough of its own.[7]

Chapter 8
SUICIDE
AND OTHER
HANGUPS

Of all the infirmities we have, the
most savage is to despise our own being.

— Michel de Montaigne

Surviving obviously cannot coexist with suicide. I mean suicide ranging from the single, deliberate, positive act of putting a pistol to your head to the multiple, quasi-deliberate acts of abandoning the will-to-live, as in *anorexia nervosa* or alcoholism.

The minute we are conceived, we are old enough to die and, before too long, we discover this fact — often to our surprise and shock. We soon learn that living is a matter of choosing to continue to live, a choice we retain for the rest of our lives. "The thought of suicide is a great consolation: by means of it one gets successfully through many a bad night," said Nietzsche.

Real death is, of course, nobody's thought. It is an objective event, a happening outside of human consciousness. What happens within consciousness is not death but morbidity — the *thought* of death, with its related thoughts of aging, suffering pain, dependency, loss of faculties, becoming a "vegetable."

Such thoughts can be produced at any age and indeed often are: The fifteen-year-old can be as morbid as the octogenarian — and just as suicide-prone.

A recent book entitled *Common Sense Suicide*[1] argues the "right" of "older people" to take their own lives. It really is arguing something prior — the right of such people to their thoughts about aging, weakening and dying until, captured by the morbidity of it all, they embrace suicide as some old, familiar friend.

Actually, older people are no more required by life or circumstances of age or consciousness to produce morbid thoughts about "growing old" than is anybody else. If anything, people of considerable years are more apt to have acquired the quintessential wisdom about life, *that it is to be lived rather than thought about,* as more than one sage has pointed out. Operationally, that means to understand that (a) all real time is now time, and (b), what is produced by and in consciousness in that now time determines the quality of your life.

The author tells us that older people have become "obsolete": "Reverence for old age is based in part on the days when the few elders who survived were the repository of the tribe's or clan's knowledge or skills. Their remembrance of events and tales of their own elders provided a comforting continuity. They were prized for their discernible value." This, she tells us, is no longer the case since, "Today we take our history from books or films, and our skills from vocational training rather than from elder craftsmen."[2]

No one is arguing that wisdom comes automatically with the piling up of years. The notion of old, therefore wise, was surely a foolish notion in any age. Yet, because the seasoned wisdom we are talking about is *sometimes* found in the old and *never* in the young (unless carefully instructed by their seniors), the argument about the obsolescence of the elder makes no sense. Thus, Bernard Berenson at ninety, a self-described "beggar with a tin cup," held out to anyone with unwanted minutes to give away.

Rather than arguments for the right to suicide, older people are better served with encouragement to use each moment of their lives — for *all* of their life — wisely. And, when encouragement is not enough, with instruction on how this is to be done.

The author writes: "....old people are notoriously cantankerous and difficult at times. Allow us to shed some of our worst *fears* [italics mine] of pain and disability, of isolation and loneliness, of loss of our functions, loss of our minds, loss of any shred of dignity. Let us shed those and we might be much, much easier to live with while we decide to live."[3]

Notice that the author is complaining about her *fears,* about her unperceived self-productions. Essentially she is begging others for permission *to stop doing something to herself!* What irony!

She needs and will get no permission from anyone to do what she wants with her own life, including ending it. And, unless she values it herself, no one will be able to do it for her.

People who take their own lives — and this may be as many as 100,000 a year in the United States, according to experts — clearly decided that their suffering wasn't worth it. Yet, if they had stuck it out, they might well have discovered that they were mistaken, that their suffering *was* worth it, was in fact a kind of pure gold.

One of the great survivors of our times was the World War I flying ace, Captain Eddie Rickenbacker. He capped a long string of earlier racing car and aircraft survivals with a sensational return from twenty-four days in an open life-raft in the South Pacific during World War II. One reads his story with wonder and admiration for his indomitable will-to-live.[4]

Was it worth it? He had a large payoff of many additional years with his loved ones, friends, and associates. It taught him, among other things, to appreciate the common things of life. He writes in his autobiography that, after his rescue, he rarely passed a drinking fountain without taking a relished sip.

Surely if life may be said to have a point, the ability to relish it is that point. And that comes down to being able to relish the multifarious realities in the universe, like sky and stars, grasses and butterflies, sand and surf. Also its human inhabitants, including oneself.

The best reason for enduring one's miseries is the purely selfish (or rather, enlightened) one: Live through them somehow, and they will put you in a commanding position to savor the universe.

Surviving has its magnificent uses, uses the suicide forgoes because he sees no point in his suffering, no gain from carrying on.

Picture, if you will, Rickenbacker on that little rubber raft, able at any time to end his torment by rolling over the side into the obliging sea. He chose instead to endure, to suffer what he was powerless — short of suicide — to change, to bear his fears and bodily torments on that pitiless ocean of scorching days and bone-chilling nights, while crammed with two other men into space designed for one. Did he know, down deep, or find out only later, how sweet would be his human reward in heightened sensibility to reality? (Is this, one might well ask, the authentic religious experience?)

G. K. Chesterton once noted that bitter experiences don't necessarily make bitter people. It would seem that bitter people are forever in panicky flight from the educating embrace of the world's miseries which are trying, as it were, to give them a more enlightened perspective of the world. Good fortune of health, wealth, youth, beauty has "spoiled" them. And affliction alone can cure them. Yet they will not take the cautery of pain full in the wound to stanch and purify it. They fly from troubles to drink and drugs and suicide, protesting loudly at life's cruelty and God's gratuitous hatred of them.

Suicide is a cop-out, a desertion of the real order of things into the imagined consolations of oblivion. The humans who leap from bridges to their mortal end are simply throwing away the marvelous potentials for enriched living on the other side of their suffering. They need to give themselves the gift of more time in order to realize that, their opinions to the contrary, the universe knows what it is doing.

> Lord of happenings, & little things,
> muster me westward fitter to my end —
> which has got to be Your strange end for me —
> and toughen me effective to the tribe enroute.[5]

Chapter 9
THE GREAT FEAR

Aye, but to die, and go we know not where,
To lie in cold obstruction and to rot.
This sensible warm motion to become
A kneaded clot and the delighted spirit
To bathe in fiery floods, or to reside
In thrilling region of thick-ribbed ice —
To be imprisoned in the viewless winds,
And blown with restless violence round about
The pendent world, or to be worse than worst
Of those that lawless and incertain thought
Imagine howling — 'tis too horrible!
The weariest and the most loathed worldly life
That age, ache, penury, and imprisonment
Can lay on nature is a paradise
To what we fear of death.

— William Shakespeare

It is because of soliloquies like this put in the mouth of the seemingly doomed Claudio that "Measure for Measure" is called a *dark* comedy. Is that any way to treat an audience which comes to be distracted by merriment and light touches, and then is reminded bluntly, albeit poetically, of "The Great Fear"? Why, it is enough to prompt any self-respecting, paying customer to demand his money back. "Those who want speeches on death can take themselves to 'Hamlet' or to 'Coriolanus,' or to other morbid exercises about man's doomed condition. I, "insists our unhappy theater-goer," came to be amused, to be diverted."

The Great Fear. The fear of death. All living things must die, but humans *know* it, must live with that knowledge daily, must bear its mystery, its unacceptability, its certainty. Is it any wonder that the subject of death is taboo in polite company, that copious human energy goes into "schemes of amnesia," which strive to push The Great Fear into Siberias of consciousness — only to have some poet-playwright, imitating life, spoil the party?

The Great Fear. Aristotle, writing in his *Ethics* about courage, shows us why Shakespeare has "spoiled the party:"

> With what sort of terrible things, then, is
> the brave man concerned? Surely with the
> greatest; for no one is more likely than he
> to stand his ground against what is awe-inspiring.
> Now death is the most terrible of all things; for
> it is the end, and nothing is thought to be any
> longer either good or bad for the dead.[1]

Yet why blame Shakespeare or anyone else for ruining things for us? Such writers only tell the truth about life. If the Bard of Avon is a great dramatist, it is because life itself presented him with its own Great Drama, something which he only partly captured, despite his genius. He is great, but the Natural Spectacle of Life and Death is immeasurably greater.

Such a Natural Spectacle strikes the undistracted human consciousness with enormous force. On what he supposes is his last night on earth Claudio gives vent to his fears: ". . . to die, and go we know not where . . . to rot . . . this sensible warm motion to become a kneaded clot . . . 'tis too horrible!" Almost cruelly, Shakespeare here gives us a taste of what our real death will be like when, like poor Claudio, we must finally *live* it: it has at last come for us (or for someone we love). True, it is a mere taste of death, vicariously served up in Shakespeare's theater, but if we are closely attending, it rips away our euphemisms and makes us say in our deepest soul, "Yes. That is what it will be like!"

The fear of death is the Great Fear not only because death is "the most terrible of all things," but because every other fear, whether of failure or of rejection or of illness or of going crazy or of disgrace or of old age or of heights and of flying, or whatever, is a species or variant of it. This means that if we succeed in understanding the fear of death, we will know much about other fears and perhaps something about life itself.

Being afraid is natural to living creatures: without it there would be no drawing away from danger, no flight from the fatal consequences of some foolhardy action and therefore no survival. What is natural may also be necessary. Thus the creature — whether human or brute — which is afraid of water is protecting itself from death by drowning. The absolutely fearless person — Aristotle calls him "rash" — is a very poor insurance risk, someone who will surely in time, given the hazards even of ordinary life, get himself killed. Living beings keep themselves alive by responding with fear to threats against their lives in ways that prevent mortal trauma. Fear is functional. It serves a truly vital *function* — for what is more vital than preserving one's life? Such fear may be called healthy fear: it is simple, spontaneous, useful, and necessary, and it vanishes with the removal of the threat.

Yet if simple fear is functional, there can be a fear which is dysfunctional, one which disserves the living creature and defeats the salutory purpose of fear. Dysfunctional fear is complex fear, fear that arises not as a healthy response to a real and concrete threat to life and limb, but as a response to fear itself. This may be called "fear about fear," which means, literally, "to live in fear."

Brute animals experience fear but do not live in fear. They are cautious about concrete dangers but do not live in dread of attack, of being eaten, of dying. No, "fear about fear" is a human ailment, a complication which springs out of the complexities of the human spirit. It involves a "reading" on the reality of danger, is an intellectual rather than an instinctive response, a coming-to-the-conclusion that the world is a "threat." The answer it gives to Einstein's famous formulation: "The most important question is this: Is the universe friendly?" is "No!"

We do not have Einstein's unequivocal answer to his question: He found the universe mysterious, challenging, provocative of piety, but not specifically "friendly." Which is not to say he found it "dangerous": When informed by his doctors that he had a cardiac aneurysm which could kill him at any moment, he is reported to have said resignedly, "Let it happen." This suggests that he did not dread his own death, did not live in fear of it pathologically — although he may have found it "terrible" in Aristotle's understanding of the brave man. It may repay us to examine the complex fear of death — as opposed to the instinctive response to lethal danger — for a dependable answer to Einstein's question.

What does the human experience of The Great Fear tell us about the essential attitude of the universe to us? If we take the instinctive part of the Great Fear, the recoiling from life-endangering circumstance, it is clear that here the universe is out to keep us alive rather than to "do us in." Indeed, to the extent that we let our fear *instincts* guide us in dangerous situations, we can thank such instincts for keeping us alive. We must then conclude that here the universe is being friendly to us: It spawns dangers for us, but warns us against them.

Let us now consider the non-instinctive part of the Great Fear, the fear that we have called "intellectual" and specifically human.

We notice at once that intellectual fear is not an immediate response to concrete danger, but a mediated one, i.e., one that is a response to abstract danger, to a danger recognized by the mind in reflection. It is psychological rather than ontological danger, by which I do not mean less real (or more), but simply a different kind of danger. It is *mental* danger, danger which is *thought about*, danger which exists specifically in some human being's consciousness. In a word, it is "self-produced" danger.

Self-produced danger is *real* danger: It is not the kind of real danger inherent in an avalanche during a skiing trip or in a capsized boat at sea, but it is nonetheless *real*, which is to say, that it is more than nothing. It is real fear, a real experience. Intellectual fear differs from instinctive fear not in its *reality* but in its causation: *The cause of intellectual fear is the mind itself.*

Instinctive fear is looking at the territory; intellectual fear is looking at the map of the territory. So long as fear is instinctive and operates as a reflexive response to danger, it needs no analysis — it is simple, normal, unerring. It is natural, necessary, and healthy: it serves a vital survival function. This cannot be said equally of intellectual fear, although even here there are normal, healthy states. Some people, perfectly normal, are so fearful of fire for example, — perhaps they have been burned, seen or read something harrowing involving it — that they are always on the alert about its dangers. They have a kind of nervous fear of it, are good customers for smoke detectors, and have their eye on the exit in crowded assemblies. Such people are not disabled by their fear, not kept at home by it, and often escape tragedies to which the devil-may-care types fall victim. Such fear, while subject to scorn as "nervous Nellie-ism," is often honored in the breach; it is perceived as sane and praiseworthy after some public fire claims hundreds of lives, as it is said, "needlessly."

But there is a species of intellectual fear that is genuinely abnormal, indeed, pathological. This is when fear has caused dysfunction and disablement, when it has become a burden to no purpose, when it has reduced the person to a "walking corporation of fears." One now has become over-ridden, a host parasitized, indeed, eaten alive by nameless, inchoate fears which presage the breakdown and death of the living organism. Fear now has not just occupied the mind, it has captured and modified it. It has colored it by its own logic and being, obliterating any other view but the one which it dictates. The person is fear-ridden, which means that the subject's own consciousness has dismounted and fear has taken the saddle. Such fear argues: "I am the way the universe is," foreclosing by such argument any contrary discussion. And what is that way? The universe is unfriendly, dangerous, deadly. Such fear presents itself to consciousness as the very landscape of reality. It is mind preempting the whole of what is, reducing it to its own scenario, in a word, "minding" the universe. It is fear fed and kept in existence by the willed attentions of consciousness. Which means that the concrete, objectively real threats to life which occur in nature have been idealized, made abstract and subjective by mental process. Particular dangers have been now made general and pervasive; local dangers have become cosmic. And if the person can flee from concrete instances of fire, can take reasonable precautions against being caught unawares, there can be no escape from "fire in the mind" by any person fully captured by his own mental productions, such that his mental productions are synonyms for himself. Such "cosmic fire" has operationally trapped the person and offers only madness or suicide as escape.

In this manner, the whole purpose and function of natural fear, whether instinctive or intellectual, has been defeated. Normality has abdicated to pathology. Health has been replaced by disease.

If this is correct, all the above applies to The Great Fear, that fear which is at the root of all the others. Thus, there is for humans not just brute animal dying with its instinctive protection of fear, but human dying with its additional knowing component. Because we are capable of knowing, we are susceptible to what might be called "diseases of knowing," resulting in fear pathology. As we have seen, in fear pathology it is the reading that the mind makes of its own contents that is decisive for the person's view of the matter. And since the contents of the mind respecting the subject of death are idealized or "cosmic," death can have only one meaning for such a consciousness: " 'tis horrible." Because such fear is steadily and inescapably *real* in consciousness, such reality dictates the way the universe is: unfriendly, lethal, unrelievedly evil. Indeed, with death threatening cosmically, totally and on every side, what other conclusion can consciousness draw?

But it is not a simple pathology, this cosmic fear of death holding sway over consciousness. We have called it complex. What complicates the matter for its victim is a common philosophical assumption about the nature of human existence. Let us pause now to examine this assumption.

One of the reasons that brute animals do not fear death, (although they instinctively recoil from dangers to their life), is that they have no concept of death *as a danger to their existence.* But then, neither do humans have such a concept: they have, rather, an *idea* of such a danger. The difference is crucial. Let me illustrate this by comparing Socrates' sentiments in the face of death as reported by Plato in *The Apology* with those of Claudio, already noted.[2] Facing their respective mortal end, Socrates is serene and unafraid, Claudio desperate and terrified. Mastering his natural instinct of recoil from an attack by the hemlock on his body, Socrates *knew* that he would soon experience death, but steadfastly generated no self-terrifying *idea* in his consciousness. Thus his serenity. In contrast Claudio, as indicated by his soliloquy, ideologized his death *by thinking about it.* The speech reports his thoughts: of going he knew not where, of rotting, of bathing in fiery floods, etc. With such terrifying thoughts, is it any wonder he was terrified? If Socrates had fear, it was concrete and instinctual: the horrid taste of hemlock, the pain of undergoing poisoning, something easily mastered, as we have said. Poor Claudio's fears were complex, instinctual mixed with cosmic. They broke his courage and soon sent him pleading to his sister to save his life by submitting to his captor's carnal desires.

But there was something else operating on both men, something even more crucial to their courage. Socrates identified himself with his non-bodily reality which was immune to harm; Claudio with a body that would "rot" and that would be "blown with restless violence." Socrates saw that he had nothing to lose by dying, since he, as he told his weeping followers in the cell, was immortal and was going to eternal bliss. Claudio feared that he would lose the "paradise" that was now his by comparison with what death would bring him. Socrates was philosophical about dying in contrast to Claudio; but then, of course, it should be remembered that Socrates was precisely a . . . philosopher.

What may be said about death and The Great Fear of it, philosophically? Many things, of course: libraries are full of musings about human dying. Such musings, however, are reducible to only two basic possibilities, oblivion or continuation. If oblivion, there then being no you to have experiences, death will bring deliverance — a negative one. If continuation, will it be the kind of torment that Claudio feared, or will it be the bliss that Socrates anticipated? Additionally, will human merit be a factor, as at least Socrates believed ("No evil can happen to a good man.")?

Clearly, if death leads to continuation in torment — quite independently of individual merit — the universe has answered Einstein's question for you: It is unfriendly, indeed, malevolent. You will be damned no matter what you do.

Under such circumstances, there can be no gain in the fearful anticipation of death. As the Spartan soldier was wont to say, "If you have to go through the stream, it doesn't matter whether it is hot or cold." The Epicurean code then comes to the fore: Eat, drink and be merry now: tomorrow we die (and are in torment). More to the point, *live as long as you can. Do nothing to hurry your death.*

Again, clearly, if death leads to bliss — merit having no bearing — the universe is friendly (*Pace*, Einstein).

But if the condition after death is decided by merit, the Great Question is this: *Is willful suicide going to put me in Hell?* And there can be no doubt that the very fear of such a possibility has stayed the hand of many a would-be suicide. Such fear, it must be said, favors (is friendly to) life, much after the manner of instinctive fear, as seen earlier; indeed it acts as a very strong natural complement to it.

Thus, for all circumstances involving continuation after death, the fear of death acts to *perpetuate* life, is friendly to the living creature. It is even friendly, at least negatively, in the case of oblivion after death. So that philosophical analysis has given us the answer to Einstein's "Most important Question." The universe cunningly tries to keep us alive, to protect us, as it were, from our follies. As R.D. Laing has written; "There is nothing to be afraid of. Nothing."[3] And Herman Hesse:

The dream of death is only the dark smoke under which the fires of life are burning.

Chapter 10
BEING BORED

*My religion consists of a humble admiration
of the illimitable superior spirit who reveals himself
in the slight details we are able to perceive
with our frail and feeble mind.*

— Albert Einstein

Being bored is an unnatural state. If the world were bored with itself, without question it would not now exist. And a quick inspection of any part of the natural world shows how unbored the world is: birds wake to song, plants bloom shamelessly, crickets will not be still, planets hurry on their courses, the sun and all stars of the cosmos explode continuously in excited splendor.

Well, you say, the fact still remains that I am bored. Bored to death. The universe may be fascinated with itself, but I am neither a sun, a bird, nor a cricket. For one thing, I have an imagination and a memory, a mind which can conceive of a thousand things I would rather be doing than working at this repetitive job, looking at the same old face each morning in the mirror, chit-chatting with the same people. And, you say, frankly it does no good to tell me I *shouldn't* be bored, as though I could shed my boredom like an unwanted skin just by willing it. Furthermore, calling my boredom unnatural will only make me feel guilty about it . . . and do nothing to rescue me from it.

Fair enough. It does absolutely no good to preach against boredom as on some moral subject. Yet surely is it accurate to say that boredom is an unnatural state. The very words "bored to death" indicate that strongly.

No living thing can remain indifferent to its own death. The instinctive and natural action is to contrive an escape, to fly from what threatens its life. And the bored-to-death can think of nothing else but escape almost as if their lives depended upon it.

In a certain very important sense if you are bored, your life *does* depend upon escaping your boredom. Biologically and psychologically, boredom echoes in your body and takes its toll in blunted responses and dampened vital resources — the alarm has already sounded: Retirement is a sentence of premature death for millions in our society.

There is, in fact, no real way to escape from the "boring now." To what can you escape? To yesterday? But yesterday is gone, and the most vivid memory cannot bring it back as more than a pale ghost. To tomorrow? There is an old wisdom about the uncertainty of tomorrow's chickens. Clearly, it is most unwise to trade what now is for what only may be.

On the other hand it is not unnatural to yearn for an improvement in your affairs, for a shift to a better time. Nor is it unprofitable to do so. Milton, grown blind, wrote poignantly of what might be termed "fruitful waiting":

> Thousands at his bidding speed
> And post o'er land and ocean without rest;
> They also serve who only stand and wait.[1]

To wait fruitfully is not to dream away the now, to brood about its dismalness, to protest its unacceptability, all the hallmarks of being bored. It is to cherish the now as the delivery room of all that will be. And while one hopes for the best, one wastes no time fretting over what may be considerably less than that. One waits expectantly, but not morbidly; hopefully, but not oblivious to what the present itself has to offer.

The one-who-waits in this manner does not merely wait: he is alive to all that the world is currently offering for his eye and ear and nose.

"What are you looking at so eagerly?" asks the bored-to-death.

"There. Do you see it? That spider busy with his web; that tuft of smoke trailing off in the distance. Do you smell that fragrance of lilacs in the air? And before that . . . "

But the bored-to-death has already seen smoke coming from chimneys, and spiders on walls, and smelled lilacs, and these are only three in a long, long list of things which will not be noticed or missed. A bird on a limb? A face in the crowd? A rustle in the trees? How boring!

No, there is no escape from the now into a better time, as the bored-to-death sooner or later find out. Happiness must be found now, if it is to be found at all. It is the now which is the time of everything real and exciting and natural in the universe. It is this moment, properly seen and used, which provides the only escape from boredom which is genuinely possible.

> To see a World in a grain of sand
> And a Heaven in a wild flower,
> Hold Infinity in the Palm of your hand
> And Eternity in an hour.[2]

Chapter 11
LIVING
YOUR
REAL LIFE

We take our mortal momentary hour
With too much gesture....

— Robinson Jeffers

Many people think as though their lives depended upon it — that is to say their many "lives" as social beings. These "lives" depend upon thinking about them for a very simple reason: Whatever reality the "lives" have is the result of thinking. That is why when the stockbroker goes broke or the artist is rejected by the critics, one hears him say, "My life is over." It is as though he were telling himself continuously, "Think, or you shall not be!"

You are, let us say, a colonel in the army. You were duly promoted to that high military rank after years of slow, earned advancement. You have in your possession the validating documents, you draw the pay, you command the authority that goes with your rank. Yet for all that heavy social confirmation, your colonelcy is simply not "out there," say, like a tree with all its objectivity and solidity. Your colonelcy obviously is real but strangely and unsubstantially so. Let us now examine a colonelcy to determine how real it is.

While there is no such thing as a colonelcy in the way that a tree may be called a thing, it would be fallacious, we say, to call it unreal. Since by reality we mean that which is more than nothing, it is clear that a colonelcy is real since it is more than nothing, indeed a good bit more, as every colonel in the world would insist. But exactly what kind of a reality is it?

It will help to recall the process by which you became a colonel: One day you were officially promoted. "You are now a colonel," the President and the Congress, the Department of Defense and the whole of American society in effect said to you. "You may now think of yourself as a colonel."

Think of yourself as a colonel — the words are instructive. They indicate that your colonelcy is the creation of human thought, first of all that of certain civil authorities and then of you. Yet it is an invitation not to a single act of thinking but to a continuity of thought over an indefinite period, surely no mean task. How will you accomplish it?

In the first place you must think your colonelcy correctly to remain one. As a colonel you will have to walk the narrow path between taking yourself too seriously (fanaticism) and not taking yourself seriously enough (frivolity). To do this you must frequently strike the right note to balance off the times when you will be "off-key."

As a colonel you will have many things to think about, including your colonelcy. It is not the colonel in you that waters the lawn, goes to the polls, dances with your wife. The world expects more of you than being a colonel, and you must lay your colonelcy aside frequently and graciously. You must hide your serious intention to be a colonel, sublimate it very often in your life — all while keeping your life as a colonel alive. How will you do this? Since your life as a colonel is entirely a function of human thought, that life is only as solid or as real as the thought itself.

Fortunately, you will have some powerful help. Somehow, strangely, thoughts seem to obey an inertial law just like Newton's moving bodies,[1] and your colonelcy has that law to help you maintain it. Yet a thought set into motion by an individual or even by a whole society has a multitude of frictional forces always at work on it. Once launched by powerful social forces, your colonelcy will be propagated through time until or unless revoked by some equally powerful retarding force such as demotion or death, or by some positive action by you, such as resignation or treason. Then there are the other frictional factors: Your colonelcy will not survive aging, mental disease, or assaults on the body politic such as military defeat, constitutional overthrow, or irreversible anarchy.

It should now be clear what risks there are connected with any colonelcy: They are the risks connected with consciousness. The most positive colonelcy in the world, one that is backed up by the most dynamic and energetic individual intention and by the most imperious social force imaginable, including the most costly and compelling symbols of office, is a thing of the mind, necessarily as momentary, as insubstantial, as idiosyncratic as human thought itself. A colonelcy is as weak (or as strong) as the thinking which gives it life.

There is a problem, too, regarding your colonelcy's very reality. A colonelcy is complicated by the fact that there is the real kind and the make-believe kind. And when we say "make-believe," we are not talking about those inhabitants of asylums who are sure they are colonels — or Napoleons. We are referring to the colonels on stage, in the movies, to the colonel and his lady about whom Kipling wrote. Even these colonels are not nothing; we have no trouble recognizing them, following them in their fictional careers. We never confuse the colonel with his military inferiors at the picture show. Surely there is a kind of reality attending such colonelcies. If we grant reality to such colonels as rode horses in *Gone With the Wind*, we can hardly deny it to the colonel at the local army post. We would be forced to say that his colonelcy is *real*, even somehow more real than the movie kind.

No doubt we can grapple with the problem of a colonelcy endlessly, and tantalize ourselves just as endlessly with the mystery connected with it. What might perhaps help to clarify the problem, if not to solve it, would be to locate it.

We have already noted that a colonelcy is not "out there" like a tree. And this is true both of a make-believe colonelcy and a real one. Each reality has its own respective location; the tree is in the garden, the movie-colonel is on the screen, and the real one is in the consciousness. In saying this, we somehow locate the place of each reality's occurrence, providing a piece of very useful information for our inquiry.

We mentioned the tree and the movie-colonel only as a reference — it is the real colonelcy which concerns us now, particularly the question of its reality. And we have located it in consciousness. In whose consciousness? Obviously first in yours. Then, well, in everyone's, at least potentially, invited as they are by insignia and uniforms to produce your colonelcy within them.

We come back then to the very first sentence of the chapter: *Many people think as though their lives depended upon it.* And you are one of those, if your colonelcy is your real life. It is lived at risk, as we have seen; you would do well to learn the art of surviving the "death" of your colonelcy, a "death" that could have "fatal" consequences for you unless you have made alternate arrangements.

What are those consequences? It all depends upon how identified, how invested you are in that "life" emotionally. Clearly, if all you have going for you is your "life" as a colonel (or as stockbroker or artist), the "death" of it can "wipe you out." You would need to move quickly to develop another life, a more real one.

Notice we say *you* must move quickly, for there is a you, a person, a reality who has survived the social death. That "wiped out" person's heart is still beating, his brain still operating, his being still in existence. Nietzsche noted this fact very well when he observed that he who despises himself nonetheless esteems the despiser within himself.

Real life is not discovered through thought. Nor is it constituted by thought, as demonstrated by the fact that it is "there," antecedent to and independent of thought. As the poet Robert Burns said, "A man is a man for a' that," "a' that" being the heap of social forms and structures of thought we pile on him.

Real life is a unique form of life compared to all the other "lives" humans lead, an exemplar which those other "lives" strive unsuccessfully to imitate. It is responsible for those other forms in the way that the host is responsible for the parasite which it supports. And yet that analogy limps badly when pushed too far, because the biological parasite is a separate and separable, if not self-sufficient, organism. Not so the "lives" that thinking produces. A colonelcy is the product of the thinking human being, and although a distinct state of being, has no existence, as we have seen, apart from thought.

Real life, then, is neither discovered by nor constituted through thought. It is wholly outside the ken of thought, wholly escapes being grasped by thought, has nothing in common with it. This is the reality which needs no thinking it to make it be, the reality which is the foundation upon which all other "lives" are built. This is the life outside the quotation marks, the life which-takes-care-of-itself. In short, it is the life of the real you. Living *that* life, you will find that the "death" of your colonelcy or of any other "life" will not mean "the end of you." Living that life you will survive every "death."

Dark, dark my light, and darker my desire.
My soul, like some heat-maddened summer fly,
Keeps buzzing at the sill. Which I is I?
A fallen man, I climb out of my fear.
The mind enters itself, as God the Mind,
And one is One, free in the tearing wind.[2]

Chapter 12
SOCIAL ENVY

Thou shalt not covet thy neighbor's goods.

— The Tenth Commandment

There is just no way in which everybody can be king, queen, prince, president, or heir to a fortune. At least not in physical fact. The crown rests uneasily on the monarch's head more because of social envy than of perhaps any other single cause. "Why should he be so privileged? Why not me?" the social revolutionary asks.

Such a complaint is understandable, predictable. Self-love is so intense a passion in the individual heart that everyone wants the best for himself, deeming himself more real and therefore more eligible than anybody.

Each person has the immediate experience only of his own reality: that of others he reasons to. Putting oneself in another's shoes requires a certain effort, that is why it is an admonition. And frequently that effort is never made: others become at best mere images on one's personal viewing screen, extinguishable by the equivalent of a flip of the dial.

Depriving the reigning monarch of his crown and having it conferred on oneself may be reasonable only to oneself, but that is enough from one's own point of view. Others do not sympathize with it — each person, including the king, is out for his own prospering — but social matters get decided not by the arguments of ego but by powerful conventions. In a world of competing but numerically equivalent egos, something other than egoistic desire tips the scale for the socially favored, like birth, talent, beauty, or good fortune.

It is at best a stand-off, a very uneasy one, for the individual ego is not so easily overridden. Given an opportunity to improve itself, for example in a revolution, it quickly enlists, even when the reward is not to be in material coin: The fall of eagles helps the sparrow to a prouder view of itself.

Revolutions are nasty business: A lot of blood gets shed, and when the smoke of guns and bombs clears, there is always a new "king" on his throne, though sometimes his title gets sanitized for "democratic" purposes. Better some other way to quiet the egoistic urgings and hurt pride of that great majority of people who in social terms are all but anonymous — though not to themselves, of course. But is there some other way?

There is. It is really the only practical way to distribute safely the glory that every human ego restlessly craves. Yet it is the way that does *not* follow the route of the frustrated who must console himself as best he can with the "sourness" of the grapes beyond his reach.

For the "grapes" of privilege are, in everyman's view, well worth having and this accounts for all the discontent, all the social envy. "Ah, to live in a palace, with a beautiful queen, amidst chandeliers, marble staircases, footmen in attendance, the royal treasury open to my needs!" says Everyman.

Social envy is generated by a belief in the singular advantage of the legal, physical possession or ownership of material goods. Under such a condition, it is held that the king or millionaire "has" the palace, the jewels, the riding stables, the millions, the townhouse, the private plane, the Rolls-Royce automobile, and the non-king and non-millionaire have not. Yet, actually, material possessions are "owned" by the privileged in a most ambivalent and tenuous way. Every "ownership" is subject to the attritions of time, the risks of radical political change, the dangers of theft or expropriation, the loss of the very sensory power to experience and enjoy them, etc. What good are jewels to a blind king, rich food to a diabetic Croesus? The jaded sybarite has a problem with his possessions that mere physical ownership will not solve: He, like everyone else, is subject to that strange paradoxical law, viz., that one must lose what one has in order really to find it.

Physical possession or ownership has its limitations, and they should give the envious non-possessor pause: The very thing that provokes so much envy and social resentment has small power to satisfy the human heart.

There is another way to possess a thing — it is by discovering that one possesses it already; that really no attempt at "possession" need be made; and that such possession is the only real one there is — all others being a materialist illusion based on the false two-fold belief that physical possession is the only real possession and that the self and the physical body are identical.

The enlightened man believes neither and therefore is free of social envy. It is not his virtue which restrains his greed and egoistic passion — it is his awareness that he need not crave what he already possesses. He does not see himself limited to some fixed material point, confined in some cubicle of flesh called his "body." He realizes that his is an inclusive rather than an exclusive existence, because of the outreach of his existence. He doesn't understand himself as somebody who lacks some property "outside" of himself: he realizes that he actually contains all places and therefore all things which occupy these places.

Egoism is a state of consciousness which inevitably and unavoidably produces discontent and unhappiness. This is because it is an impoverished state, one felt keenly by its host, who ceaselessly struggles to break out of it. But it is a "break-out" conceived materialistically, for the egoistic imagination is a radically material one: It can only think of relieving its "poverty" by material appropriation, by physical acquisition. It covets its neighbor's goods (and frequently his wife as well). It wants relief from the alarming state of having so little. Even the egoistic king is never satisfied and, under the cover of the praiseworthy drive for "security of the kingdom," reaches out for more and more material possessions. The kingdom under such a king churns with unrest, its people led on to hardship, suffering, and death by the falsest claims to sovereignty, while the gap between the grandeur and nobility of the king and the commonness and expendability of the commoners widens. And worst of all, such royal egoism has a way of infecting the whole kingdom with its deadly disease.

It is all a madness and doomed to ludicrous failure: Sooner or later, each individual who conceives himself as a material self is lead to weariness and frustration. "What went wrong?" the continually frustrated ego asks. "I did everything I was supposed to do; I acquired what was my dearest heart's desire, all to no avail. I am as poor as when I began."

Egoism is true madness: It is an attempt to redesign the universe based on a fundamental misunderstanding of it. It is the enunciation of an "I" which falls deaf on the living ear of the universe. It speaks to itself and the words reverberate down the long caverns of the mind of the egoist, returning its charming but hollow echo. The universe is not brute matter, which is to say, it is not limited in any of the ways it seems to be to a materialized consciousness. What the egoist does not see is the reality of the world. He sees only kinds of things, i.e., limitation. But reality is not finally any kind of thing — *except the kind of thing which is real.* Things are only superficially this or that. Because each thing is real, it has a living, continuous connection with every other kind of thing. This is what makes it all a universe. And that is the great and indispensable task of the human consciousness — to see that truth and to apply it boldly, first of all to itself. Until that is done, there is no peace, no sense of fulfillment, no happiness.

There is no need for pessimism about this process — reality takes care of itself unerringly: madness and foolishness do not prevail. What things *really* are — and *that* they are — is not countermanded by any human mind with mad designs on the world. Human consciousness is, in fact, not confined to a bag of skin; it outreaches to the whole of reality and takes it in as its own. The enlightened person understands this truth; that is why he is not tempted to envy about social privilege. He sees that what the privileged *really* have, he has, too. And this extends in a very real way to their material possessions as well. He does not feel poor, since he knows he is real — and there is no greater wealth than that!

Envy is a peculiarly selfish vice. It arises when the mind has become engaged with its own characterizations of reality and has turned its attention to them in place of reality itself. These characterizations present themselves to the mind as categories of thought. One of those categories of mind is "I," the self, the solitary unit contained within the perimeter of this loop of skin, particular and materialized in space. Egoism is an invention of mind. It is constructed from impressions gathered by a consciousness operating on materialistic assumptions. Like every assumption, it originates in a "leap" from sense experience, but in the case of the egoistic mentality, from a sense experience which is already prejudiced by material considerations.

Social envy is basically insatiable: It is consciousness warring against the rest of reality. It is reality perceived through the lens of abstract social ideas which continuously invite the subject to utopian experiments and assaults against a "resisting, uncooperating and even malevolent universe." Such a consciousness cannot be improved by some "better ideology," by more "scientific" thinking, by any materialist rectification of consciousness. It can be improved only by enlightenment about the nature of reality itself.

What therefore is enlightenment? It is the singular corrective to the old debility and vice of human secular consciousness. It is basically an intuitive insight into the connectedness and unity of all things, a realization in real time of the exquisite appropriateness of every event, of the radical and essential spirituality, indeed, the divinity of all being. It is an oceanic consciousness that sees through the seeming material limitations of things (really of thoughts about things), one that therefore has no trace of any social envy bred by egotism. It does not begrudge the king his role in society, his palaces, or his privileges, precisely because no part of the reality of the cosmos excludes the enlightened consciousness. Thus the enlightened human being has no sense of being deprived, of being a victim, of being rejected by or alienated from the universe itself. He is not the captive of any materialist assumption, does not see himself as confined to a perimeter of being, as defined by any conception of self which is exclusive of any reality in the universe. Reality does not require him to find his abode in the confines of his own mental self-productions. Rather reality invites him to a universality of view, or rather, simply to be real.

With enlightenment there is no king to envy, no Joneses to keep up with. The universe does not threaten — it unfolds more and more of its secrets, more and more of its fitness and splendor. The true self of the person has come out of the baleful shadow-world of the ego into the full sunshine of the normal, vital, healthy personality.

Chapter 13
ON GOOD AND EVIL

All is best, though we oft doubt
What the unsearchable dispose
Of Highest Wisdom brings about.

— John Milton

In an old Chinese tale a child with a lame foot was born to a couple. "Why did this evil happen to us?" lamented the wife on seeing the child. Relatives and friends gave their condolences, but the husband said only, "Wait and see." Years passed and the baby and his playmates grew to young men. Then Mongols brought war from the North, threatening to breach the Great Wall. The youths of the village were conscripted into military service. Many of them were injured and killed, leaving their parents behind without sons to support them in their age and to perform the funeral rites. But the couple with the lame son were spared such sorrow. Because of his lameness, he was passed over for military service and, even though lame, was the comfort of his parents all their lives.

Lameness is evil? Poverty, blindness, cancer, old age? Wait and see.

What, you ask, a mother whose child has been killed at a school crossing must wait and see if her loss is evil? That's absurd. She grieves night and day, she has aged ten years, she will never forgive herself for being late that day to meet her child, nor will her husband. It was their only child. Not evil, you say? Not evil here and now beyond any doubt or argument? Ridiculous.

Yet, would the child unfailingly have grown up a healthy, happy and useful human being? Perhaps, but a lot of children grow up to break their parents' hearts as drug addicts, drunkards, prostitutes, felons. Can anyone deny that for such parents a loss in childhood would have spared them greater suffering later?

But, you say, that argument is still absurd. The presumption is that the child will turn out well, and as long as there is that presumption, the loss in childhood will be experienced as evil by the parents.

Let us imagine for a moment that the veil covering the child's future is pulled back for the grieving parents and they see its adult life as one of unspeakable misery. Assuming they believe the vision, are they not immediately consoled in their loss? Are they not now rendered able to accept it, even to rejoice in it, whereas before the vision their loss was a cruel and unrelieved tragedy for them?

You say, under the conditions I describe, yes. But such a vision is never available to sorrowing parents, and therefore the argument is academic. To which I respond, true, but at least the hypothesis of the future vision illustrates the need for caution in assigning the label "evil" to events immediately, and the usefulness of a "wait and see" attitude toward them.

A commonplace view of evil holds that it serves no useful purpose, that it is utterly irredeemable, an ill wind that blows absolutely no good. Evil is to be conquered, stamped out, driven back to the hellish places that give it being in the first place. And so great campaigns in society are launched to defeat evil, whether it be poverty, inflation, disease, or crime. The politician who runs on the platform that a little crime keeps the police on their toes, that a little poverty gives the virtuous charitable opportunities, or that a little prostitution provides an outlet for man's libidinous urges can expect to be roundly defeated at the polls. He would have committed the unforgivable sin of conceding a place to evil in the world, of inviting the Devil to roam about in his cunning livery, devouring the weak and unsuspecting. It is bad enough that evil has already such a powerful grip on the world without extending an open invitation to it and greasing the axles of its progress. There is a great fear that evil will take over the world unless fought at every turn with energetic public zeal. We say "public" pointedly because the private interest in repelling evil is often quite another matter; here evil is not so easily mastered. It has surprising strength and often makes a mockery out of our sincerest resolutions, mere dikes of sand thrown up to contain a tidal wave of dark desires, illicit impulses, and unholy temptations. We discover elements of irreducible rascality both in ourselves and in others which would consternate us more if we did not find such elements not only amusing but also somehow socially useful. We are proud that we are not bluenoses, stuffed shirts, prigs, Puritans, and other such socially tiresome types. Being thought a hypocrite is not deemed so bad as being thought a killjoy.

What, then is evil? It has no legitimate place in orthodox Western theology's theory of the true nature of God, which holds the doctrine of the absolute polarity of good and evil, the utter irreconcilability of Christ and Satan. Yet, it has an active and valued place in all religious mythology, including the Christian.[1] The human understandably dreads its arrival on his doorstep. There can be some comfort, surely, in the realization of what mythology, that "nearest approach to absolute truth," in the words of Ananda Coomaraswamy, makes clear about the role of evil in the universe. It is a point of view that is further corroborated by the universal testimony of the mystics of all faiths, namely, that evil does have a place in the divine plan. Which is not to say that good and evil, as concepts of human understanding, are invalid; it is just that they must not be viewed as the way the world finally is.

> The old order changeth, yielding place to new;
> And God fulfills himself in many ways
> Lest one good custom should corrupt the world.[2]

Chapter 14
GOD'S
PREDICAMENT

*"It's nothing to belong, but
It's Hell not to."*

— A Member of the American Academy of Science

There ought to be a way, speaking ideally, in which having something is as good as not having it is bad. Take eyesight as as example: It is a magnificent blessing, yet one which tends to go unappreciated by the sighted. Let blindness strike — or even the threat of it — and the miracle and joy of being able to see immediately and powerfully flood the consciousness. Alan Watts tells us why this paradoxical fact of human experience occurs:

> Normal human consciousness always depends on contrasts, whether in space or in time, and tends to ignore what is constant even though it provides the necessary background for the perception of change.[1]

Watts, of course, is right. Humans do need contrast in order to live properly human lives. This means more than vegetable or animal functioning — it means human consciousness, the state of being aware with reflective intelligence. And even more than this, it means the state of a *relishing* awareness or intelligence.

What is the good, humanly speaking, of having such things as life, health, material possessions, and sight, if there is no savoring of them?

It is said that the blind man wants nothing but his sight. This is in marked contrast to the lengthy list of desires of the sighted man, for whom the possession of his sight is almost beneath his notice. True, he is the active beneficiary of his sight, but, if measured by the actual time spent relishing his power to see, unappreciatively so. From the blind man's standpoint, the sighted man is wealthy beyond measure; from his own, he fails to perceive this and instead focuses on acquisitions whose comparative triviality the blind man sees clearly.

The sighted man needs contrasting experience if he is to savor his sight, and the very best avenue to this, blindness, would also plunge him into darkness and the misery of loss. He has a predicament and, as we are going to see, it comes from the larger "predicament" of God.

One of the continuing chores of the practicing theologian is repeating an explanation for why a good and powerful God would permit evil in his creation. As Albert Camus once pointed out:

> For in the presence of God there is less a problem of freedom than a problem of evil. You know the alternative: either we are not free and God, the all-powerful, is responsible for evil. Or we are free and responsible but God is not all powerful. All the scholastic subtleties have neither added anything to nor subtracted anything from the acuteness of this paradox.[2]

Here Camus is challenging the view that evils such as blindness and death *are* reconcilable with a good, all-powerful God; if the Schoolmen of the Middle Ages couldn't do it, he is saying, why, it can't be done.

Camus' difficulty arises from his definition and understanding of God. Once God's nature is defined a certain way, as He Who Is, the difficulty disappears.[3] This definition means that such a God cannot create non-being; and this fact has an immediate impact on His power. He cannot create a being equipped with the contrasting state of non-being. Thus He cannot create a sighted person who is also blind. Simply put, such a God cannot contradict His own fiats of existence. •

It is possible to sympathize with God's "predicament," precisely because each of us shows the effect of that "predicament" in his own life, indeed, suffers from it. We ought to relish our existence, our life, our bodies, our sight, but we do not. Not really. The fault is not ours — nor, indeed, God's. The "fault" is in the Principle of Non-contradiction.[4]

Because of this principle, God cannot "afford" to give us creatures too much — it would spoil and corrupt us hopelessly. As the Arab proverb says: "Sunshine all the time makes a desert." And for us, an unshadowed existence, good as it might seem to the imagination and to the heart's desire, would be a metaphysical calamity. We would be rendered insufferably complacent and boundlessly unappreciating. The God Whose very nature is To Be sees this perfectly — and acts accordingly, sending shadows into our lives repeatedly: enough to stir us, trouble us, sadden and anger, even madden us — in order to wake us up from slumbering contentedly in the wealth of our existence. Some poets have seen this clearly:

> Is my gloom, after all,
> Shade of His hand, outstretched caressingly?
> "Ah, fondest, blindest, weakest,
> I am He Whom thou seekest!"[5]

And, by a more recent poet:

> But the prettiest fall of all
>   is my own in a gesture of love
>   as I arc through the heaven of death
>   and the angels blow my body on,
>   and I head for the heart of a girl
>   on the soft white breast of the world.[6]

As have, predictably, some theologians:

> There is no evil before God, since a good purpose is served even by that which appears bad. In the life of the human body pleasure and pain, the impetus to life and its restraint and inhibition form a necessary contrast, making for health; so, in the moral order of the universe, each being who battles with evil receives new strength for the unfolding of the good. The principle of holiness . . . transforms and ennobles every evil.[7]

And one from an earlier century, whose *Confessions* are a classic of spiritual psychology:

> To Thee be praise, glory to Thee, Fountain of mercies. I was becoming more miserable, and Thou nearer.[8]

Theologians insist that the freedom of this Biblical God is absolute. This, of course, is true, but it must be properly understood. God is only free within His own Law of Non-contradiction, within the "limits" of His own nature. Actually, such a God as this has no limits. The reason for this is that there is nothing to limit Him. Or rather, the only "thing" which could possibly limit Him, both logically and ontologically speaking, would be nothingness. Nothingness, however, can have no limiting power. The God Who Is has no limits because being has no limits. What, after all, could limit being? Non-being is the only possible candidate, and this candidate precisely is not. How, then, does he create beings who, like us, are limited? A fair question — one that has exercised the great metaphysicians of the world through history in what has come to be called "The Problem of the One and the Many."[9] Has the Problem ever been solved? If at all, not by discursive thinking but by mystical insight, by what is called in the West an ecstasy or, in Eckhart, "a little point," and in the East by a *satori, kensho, samadhi,* etc. On this D.T. Suzuki, the famed Buddhist scholar, has written:

> "A little point" left by God corresponds to what Zen Buddhists would call *satori.* When we strike the point we have a *satori.* To have a *satori* means to be standing at Eckhart's "point" where we can look in two directions: God-way and creature-way. Expressed in another form, the finite is infinite and the infinite is finite. This "little point" is full of significance and I am sure Eckhart had a *satori.*[10]

In ecstasy and *satori,* a human being sees through — breaks out of — that limitation of his creaturely existence which is the root of his predicament, his vulnerability to all the "deaths" of the human condition: He solves the Problem of the One and the Many — personally. Eckhart tries to express in words this essentially inexpressible experience:

The union of the soul with God is far more inward than that of the soul and the body. . . Now, I might ask, how stands it with the soul that is lost in God? Does the soul find herself or not? To this I will answer as it appears to me, that the soul finds herself in the point where every rational being understands itself with itself. Although it sinks in the eternity of the divine essence, yet it can never reach the ground. Therefore God has left a little point wherein the soul turns back upon itself and finds itself, and knows itself to be a creature.[11]

Then Eckhart adds an urgent footnote about the need to be in a *conscious* ecstasy, to be able to *relish* the God Who Is and, at the same time, oneself as absorbed in God:

I say that when a man looks at God, he knows it and knows that he is the knower. That is to say, he knows it is God he is looking at and knows that he knows him. Now some people wish it to appear that the flower, the kernel of blessing, is this awareness of the spirit, that it is knowing God. For if I have a rapture and am unconscious of it, what good would it do and what would it mean?[12]

If Eckhart is correct, God's "predicament" — that, in the depth of His love for us, He must provide us with exposure to non-being, more correctly, with *privations* of being, that is to say, with evils like blindness, sickness, pain, and death — is remedied by His call to union with Himself.

The cry of St. Augustine, that great wounded genius of the human spirit, is meant for all of us: "Our hearts are made for Thee, O God, and will find no rest until they rest in Thee."[13]

Chapter 15
WEEPING
WITH
ONE EYE

How can I die? I'm booked!

— George Burns

The theater is one place where humans can have their cake and eat it, too; where both what is and what is not work their simultaneous and ambivalent magic upon the consciousness. In it we are taught the way in which an experience can be both real and not real at the same time — taught the very possibility of ambivalence. The theater experience renders concrete what is first only imagined, objectifying it as a public experience. The theater-goer can now "really" experience death, not just imagine it privately; and not experience it, too, because no one is really dying on the stage.

It is because he has experienced real death outside the movie-house that the movie-goer knows what death really is, of course, and is able to distinguish the "reel" version from the real one.

Real death. Which is to say, one that is not like those at the movies. But is it real? We assume so, for what we suppose is a very good reason: There is no way to walk out on it, as we can the movie death. It is final. There is no "correcting outside order," no reality which can adjust it, so that we are free to collude or not, fictionally, in its horror, not to be smashed involuntarily by it.

As a result of experience in the theater, humans are in a position to ask these questions: Since ambivalence is a fact of theatrical reality, might it not also be one of extra-theatrical reality, of real life? Surely not. But why? Because "reel life" is different. But how? Well, it is a world of images; more than that, of images of actors. It is a shadow-world, a tissue of appearances, a pure creature of the human imagination. Yes, but is it not real, more than a mere nothing? Of course. So it is an order of reality, however shadowy, however tenuous? Yes, undeniably real — but also somehow at the same time, unreal. That is to say, ambivalent? Yes.

Thus we learn, or at least we can learn through the theater, that what we experience can be ambivalent so far as its very reality is concerned — no small or inconsequential service, surely. We become awakened to a new possibility, with vast implications for human consciousness. As a result of the theater, it is no longer necessary — or even possible — to argue that *every* experience is absolutely and finally real. The theatrical experience shows the way in which the whole universe can be theatrical, both real and not real at once. Without such experience, an awareness and understanding of ambivalence would perhaps not be possible.

Clearly the theater offers more than a fictional representation of real life — more, certainly, than mere entertainment. It provides an experience which can serve the most profound metaphysical purpose; it can be a powerful tool for discovering the great truths about the universe.

Consider the agonizing problem of human grief. There is little unrelieved grieving at the theater; there is much outside of it. What is quickly perceived as excessive, as ridiculous at the movies, is often tolerated if not defended in real life. Yet even there, grieving that is too deep, too prolonged, is rebuked. Life, it is insisted, must go on. Grieving must not be allowed to capture the person, for he is then rendered helpless. Practicality is the norm to which every passion or sorrow must ultimately bend.

Yet the exhortation in real life to stop crying about one's loss because life must go on is, at best, a grin-and-bear-it remedy. It is wise about the disabling effects of grief, but not about the causes of it. It is not a cure for it, but only a tactic for overcoming its public consequences, an admonition to get in step with that proud corps of Stoics who will not be wiped out by personal tragedy. It is an appeal to the will, not to the intellect; indeed, in the Stoic's view, there is nothing to understand about one's loss except that, grief or no, for the sake of life, one must carry on. "If you have to go through the stream, it doesn't matter whether it's hot or cold," went the Spartan soldier's wisdom, you will recall.

Such stoical advice clearly is superfluous at the movies. The solution for grief there is not to carry on bravely but to understand that it is "only a movie," that the "losses" of loved ones on the stage or screen have happened to you, but also have not.[1]

And once the ambivalency of the theatrical experience is understood, the grief is mitigated; better than that, it is cured. One eye immediately goes dry, as it were, even as the other eye continues to flow. One cries and, at the same time, one does not cry. One's grief is now within bounds and the pain from it supportable.

Similarly in real life, the cure for grief is in the wisdom of understanding that, yes, my loss happened but, no, it didn't happen either; indeed, couldn't happen. Without this understanding, without this mercy conferred by a perception of the ambivalent nature of *all* events in real life, including the tragic ones, the sufferer is exposed to all the devastating power of what is absolutely and relentlessly real. And forced to cope with it in the cold and cheerless armor of the "practical" Stoic. If one can. Is it any wonder that so few can carry it off, and escape instead to drink, to drugs, to madness or to suicide?

The Stoic carries on in loss because he *feels he must* — seeing no choice; the wise man because *he knows he can* — that he has suffered a loss "as at the theater;" that what has happened to him has also not happened to him; that only the appearance and not the substance was real. His face wears not the forced, brave grin-and-bear-it of the resigned, but the quiet easy smile of the sage, so close to erupting into laughter — seeing, as he does, the marvelous game of cosmic hide-and-seek that reality has been playing with itself. (Indeed, who else is there to play it with?) For what reason? Because it is fun. Which is why humans, too, keep going back to the theater — with all its scary happenings.

Listen to the words that the poet, James Dickey, puts in the mouth of Christ in his new book:

> Men speak of me as a man of pain and sorrow, but they have not reached the other side of God, and while I was here among you, the pain and terror were balanced by a good deal of teasing that nobody believed but God; by a great grin into nothingness, which justified everything; by a strong measure of Holy fun.[2]

It is not strange, then, that there should be such massive running to the theater by humans. For it is precisely there where the hard reality of death is mercifully blunted by ambivalence.

Death, properly understood, is seen as a good. It offers, among other benefits, that necessary contrast to life without which the latter would have no meaning. But there can be too much of a good thing, an excess of it which makes it bad. Thus it must be real enough to be good, but not so real as to be bad. It must be a reality, if it is to perform its function as antithesis to life, as the contrast by which we can realize and savor life; yet it must be unreal, too, if its very value is not to be destroyed by being overdone.

The grief that real death produces should bring tears to the eye — to one eye: the other eye should be dry, seeing as it does the unreality of the dying, realizing what Eliot has captured so beautifully that, finally:

> . . . all shall be well and
> All manner of thing shall be well
> When the tongues of flame are in-folded
> Into the crowned knot of fire
> And the fire and the rose are one.[3]

Chapter 16
GOD
AS MOVIE
DIRECTOR

If this were played upon a stage.
I could condemn it as improbable fiction.

— William Shakespeare

Let me invite you to think about God as a movie director.

Now, movie directors range in quality across a wide spectrum, from inept to inspired, and the shrewd movie-goer is guided accordingly, knowing how critical the director is to enjoyment of the film.

Yet the movie director I have in mind for you in my invitation is not D.W. Griffith, David Lean, or Akira Kurosawa, men who did and do things in a masterful, even god-like way. I have in mind no one in particular, just so long as he directs a movie. Do I mean just anyone? Yes, anyone who runs a reel of film on people whom he has directed to play roles, thereby creating an illusion. How about the story or plot, the acting, the camera work, the whole scenario? As long as some illusion is created, any quality is acceptable.

But, you rightly point out, illusion is the easiest effect of all to achieve. Just have some ham pretend to be passionately in love, involve him in a triangle and, keeping the ketchup bottle full and handy, continue cranking the camera. Why, anyone can do that!

Which is perfectly true, and the reason for it beyond dispute: On both sides of the camera humans take to illusions like the proverbial duck to water. Clearly, if humans did not easily and comfortably collude in the marvelous fictions of Rhett Butler and Scarlett O'Hara pretending to be real people, loving and hating, laughing and crying, living and dying, there could be no directors, good or bad. Even Ingmar Bergman, so justly celebrated for his directing genius, cannot make a movie for dogs. They won't, they can't collude in the fiction. Humans can and do and will. Gladly, sadly, madly. It is not simply that they will submit to playing at parts and watching them played; rather they hunger for them so much that, when there isn't a great director around to give them delicious and delightful illusions, marvelously rendered, they will gratefully accept trash, so long as it has an illusion to offer.

Humans at once know and do not know what is real. Why is that? They need to know what laughing and loving are in order to recognize their screen equivalents, but they do not know, *when caught up in a film's action,* that they are responding not to real people and their real emotions, but to pictures taken of actors and actresses. *To pictures taken of actors and actresses!* So at the movies the viewer is not just one step removed from reality but two steps. What is this but collusion in illusion — the words are remarkably close! You say the viewer *knows* it is just a story? It would be hard to tell this from the screams, the laughs, the tears that are commonplace in every movie theater. Admittedly the viewer is content to sit in his seat while the heroine is being tied to the railroad tracks, but this inaction is the result of a certain experience with film — and the ability to cancel a signal to his muscles from his illusion-captured brain in the very next instant. An unnoticed twitch is the only witness to his smothered heroism. Expose the aborigine to the first film intelligible to him and there is no such civilized twitching.

It is clear that if all life were lived in a movie, there would be no way to correct any of the illusions like the one of Pauline on the railroad tracks. The viewer would not be able to snap the illusion instantly and restrain himself, spoiling all the melo-dramatic fun. Illusions would be real to him, period. Yet the mere picture of a person and a railway track is not and can never *be* fully real, although it can definitely seem so. Our actress cannot be run over because she is really not on the tracks in the first place, but safe at home in her Hollywood mansion, martini in hand.

The imperilled figure doesn't need to be real, however, to cause the viewer anxiety and fright, that is to say, real emotional involvement. It is enough if the *pictures* are real, reasonable resemblances of real life.

Despite the considerable experience of human beings with illusions, there seems to be little impact on real life. Few ask, for example, whether real life is *really* happening. No, rather it is assumed that it is; that in real life, as opposed to reel life, people who get run over by railroad trains *really* die, having been tied there by *real* villains. In *real* life one does not cry with one eye as at the movies, but with both eyes. In real life the dead are *really* dead.

But are they? Two considerations here must surely give us pause. The first we have just been discussing, that is, the readiness with which we humans fall into illusions; the comfort we take in them; the permissiveness we have about their impact on our emotional lives; the carelessness with which they are regarded. There is a marked willingness by humans to let illusions dominate them, as though they like to be tricked and even need to be. Most humans do not greatly care to inquire about this world of dreams and fiction and thus enlighten themselves; they are content to be entertained, distracted, to be carried away into fantasy. (We except philosophers here.)

The second consideration was mentioned at the chapter's start: the possibility of God as movie director. One hears the praises of God the artist (Such a gorgeous sunset!), of God the architect (Go out beneath the stars at night and say, if you can, "There is no God!"), of God the mathematician, the law-giver, the searcher-of-hearts. Of God, the movie director? Rarely, if ever.

Yet it may be that movie-directorship is what best of all describes the divine activity. Notice that Dante's masterpiece is called *The Divine Comedy,* and that Shakespeare earned his immortality as playright/director.

God as playright/movie-director! Why not? It has been noted *ad nauseam* that "truth is stranger than fiction," that the best movies are ones based on real life, life manifesting an inventiveness, a richness, even an improbability, that is beyond the imaginings of the most fertile human imaginations. And life itself produces a gamut from "Grade C movies" that are so awful no one would believe them if they didn't happen to "Grade A movies" more magnificent in their real life unfoldment than any human director could hope to achieve, even if he had the script.

This provides an explanation for the drama of human lives, a way of accounting for good and evil in the world — requirements of any successful dramatization. Most importantly, it allows us to challenge the very reality of human experience, "correcting" it the way we might in any stage or film presentation.

Let us take just one case of human drama, a real life one, recounted in a recent book by a prison psychiatrist.[1]

Tom, one of the "deadly innocents" of the book, was starved, whipped, and isolated first by his parents and then by his uncle and aunt who took him in after he was jailed for stealing food. He finally acted when he was 14. "Tom went into the furnace room. He picked up one of his uncle's guns, and pausing only to make sure it was loaded, went upstairs to where Harry, Bertha, and Catherine were sitting at the breakfast table. Tom raised the gun, and carefully shot his uncle, then his aunt, then Catherine." The provocation? His uncle's strangling of Tom's beloved pussycat and the desecration of its grave. The cause? Dr. Gardiner, herself, wonders: "Why did it happen? Why did any of these crimes happen? What made this particular boy...commit a crime? Without a much deeper study of the unconscious drives, there is no definitive answer."

Judged by both secular and religious law, Tom did evil: He murdered another human being. He must be considered one of the "bad guys" and duly punished. What makes his story intensely dramatic, a bona fide tragedy, are the fateful circumstances surrounding it. Why was Tom so luckless to be born into a family totally unfit to bring him up properly?

It is true that Tom committed this terrible deed, but it is equally true that he did not choose to be born in the first place nor to be born into such a family. Those who insist at this point that he had free will, despite his circumstances, need to remember that his will, too, was a given, a part of his natural endowment. Once born and endowed as he was, the "play" of his life began, ending in murder.

The way to have a murder in the movies is to hire some actor to play a murderer's role, to become a "bad guy." The effort all ends as directed, A drama is produced which gives entertainment to millions, generates many jobs and much revenue. Best of all, nobody *really* gets hurt — certainly not the "murder victim." Nor does the convicted "murderer" end up in the electric chair (except on film). Oh, were real life only like that!

It is widely assumed that life is not like that, that in real life murders *really* happen and people *really* burn for committing them. Really. I say *assumed* for there is no absolute proof that this is the case, that God is not a movie-maker and the "real" is not just an appearance, skillfully made to seem otherwise. How can the matter be settled? (Notice I avoid the word "proved.") One very good way is in the manner that the famous Copernican astronomical dispute got settled, for in this affair, one should realize, there was no unassailable proof available. It will be recalled that Copernicus' shift from an earth- to a sun-centered solar system made the facts of astronomical observation more understandable, because it made them more simple. This was enough to settle the matter and to end the reign of the Ptolemaic system.

Consider with me now the marvelous simplicity that a shift from God the Judge and Lawmaker to God the Film-maker accomplishes for human understanding. It helps finally to explain Tom, the murdering boy, a bafflement to Dr. Gardiner and to her peers for all her brave talk about "unconscious drives." Under our God-as-movie-director hypothesis, Tom is playing a role in a divine script, as are the policemen who apprehend him, the jury that convicts, the judge who sentences, the warden who metes out the punishment. "Judge not," saith the Lord. And well He might, if none of the things that happen in life are happening absolutely. And who should know better than God, the movie-director?

Again, our hypothesis accommodates marvelously the problem of the goodness of God and the vast evil in the world: It regards both as really happening but really-as-in-the-movies. Just as in the moviehouse we take film experiences seriously (try laughing at a scene showing a mother weeping over her drowned son and see the reaction you get), so in real-life-as-movie everyone continues to weep over the death of loved ones, and to rejoice at a sweepstake win. But, enlightened now about its true character, we do so with a due correction, that is to say, the weeping and the laughing bring tears of sorrow or joy to only one eye.

You bad birds,
But God shall not punish you, you
Shall be with us in heaven, though less
Conscious of your happiness, probably,
But you are the fruit and jewels
Of my arrangement: O be with me![2]

Chapter 17
THE BEST OF ALL POSSIBLE WORLDS

*I no longer wished for a better world, because
I was thinking of the whole of creation, and in the
light of this clearer discernment, I had come to see
that, though the higher things are better than the lower,
the sum of all creation is better than the higher things alone.*

— St. Augustine, *The Confessions*

*All our disasters date from the moment when we began to
glimpse the possibility of "something better."*

— E. M. Cioran, *The Temptation to Exist*

*Given the things that actually exist, the universe
cannot be better, for the order which God has
established in things, and in which the good of
the universe consists, most befits things.*

— St. Thomas Aquinas, *Summa
Theologiae,* I q. 25

Could God have made a better world? No. A better world would be a more real world, and a world more real than the present one God cannot make.[1]

The idea of a better world arises only when the intelligence turns into a mind and focuses on its own ideas, an operation which necessarily fragments the universe of real being. The mind discovers kinds of things, more accurately, kinds of *thoughts* and, with them, imperfections. Thus the idea of a better world inevitably arises.

In fact, although ideas can be compared with each other and with individual things as well, reality has nothing with which it can be compared — unless it is with nothingness itself, which is hardly a candidate for comparison, being nothing. Reality cannot possibly be better than it is; it cannot possibly be different from what it is. The universe is what it is and that is all that should need to be said to settle the question of some "better" universe.

Protests will immediately arise from people who can visualize countless ways in which the universe can be improved. Such improvements would include the elimination of disease and suffering, the establishment of greater justice, love, happiness, the wiping out of ignorance, poverty, crime, etc. This would extend, if necessary, to improving either the inclination or the power of the Deity Itself to do such things for the world which would make it a better world.

A common complaint — and, given the perceptions and assumptions, an understandable if not justifiable one — is that the world is unsatisfactory: that it is far from the best of all possible worlds. This complaint is characteristically addressed to God by those who believe in Him as proof that He doesn't care about the universe, or offered as proof that He doesn't exist in the first place, whether to care or not, by those who deny His existence.

Is it possible to find in the complaint itself evidence that the complaint is wrong, that the universe is, in fact, the best it can possibly be? Let us try.

Can the best of all possible worlds co-exist with complaints about it? Or, better, would not the best of all possible worlds necessarily be free not just from complaints but from any basis for complaint?

To answer these questions, certain distinctions and quali- fications must be made. The first of these is about the scope of the complaint. There is the matter of universal and/or particular acceptance. Take universal acceptance. Is there any basis for holding that the universe is unacceptable to itself? Is there any universal complaint which is made or, indeed, can be made? Who would the universe complain to? To itself? What would that mean?

It is true that there can be particular self-complaining, as when a person views himself as "awful" or "stupid," and complains to himself about himself. It is an odd activity, but widespread for all that. And surely not some merely rhetorical exercise. How is it possible? Only because, although in one sense each person is a unity, in another sense he is not — and does not perceive himself as such. Thus, when somebody judges himself to be "awful," clearly there is the part that does the judging and the part that is deemed "awful, which is distinct from it."

If one can speak that way, there is a "higher" or more "knowing" part, i.e., the *un*awful part, and "lower," less knowing, "awful" part. There are then two "selves": the True Self and the False Self.

Now if the True Self can complain about the False Self's awfulness, to itself — perhaps proposing to do something about it, like reforming, adapting, even killing it — can the True Self complain to itself about itself? Surely not, since whatever the True Self does *is* itself, and therefore beyond complaint. It is only the lower or False Self which can do "awful" things, constituting an embarrassment and a basis for complaint for the True Self. The True Self is impeccable, masterly, all wise, all good and endlessly virtuous. It is incapable of unworthy actions.

The True Self is supremely real. As such it is infinite. It has nothing to complain about and No One to complain to. (Obviously nothingness cannot be complained to — it is precisely nothing.) And since it is supremely real, it is all there is. And since it is all there is, it is the best of all possible worlds — since the real world and the True Self of the World (which is supremely real) are not distinct from each other.

Where, then, does the notion of a better world come from?

It can arise in one "place" only and that is in consciousness. It is a proposal that is made by the mind to itself on the basis of a point of view, a certain approach to reality. It is the act of the True Self becoming a person, which is, literally, the putting on of a mask. Why does the Self put on a mask in this way? In order to create a contrast for itself. Clearly this must be a theater, a device by which the really real is ignored in favor of that which is made to appear real.

In this theater, conflict and contrasts appear all too real to the True Self in the form of "persons" who are designated to act out certain roles. It is through this theatrical device that the whole idea of a better world arises.

The limited or False Self is now in a position to do "evil," i.e., limited things, and to suffer accordingly. It is constantly in "danger" now, constantly at a loss, constantly under the hard law of contingency. It does some good things, but many things that are "awful" — which are an "embarrassment" to the True Self. Not really, of course, since it is theater.

A complaint needs to be addressed to someone by someone else, and this is what the invention of theater provides. Now the True Self can complain about the limited self to itself, about how much "better" things can and ought to be.

Now The True Self can be aware of itself, through suffering privation, pain, fear, death itself. And the mind of the limited self can experience the thrills and torments of imagining a better world than the one it presently occupies.

All this happens within the world of masks, within the theater of the mind which is invented so that the True Self may "know" itself by ignoring itself. *Know itself by ignoring itself:* What is this but paradox, a cosmic sleight-of-hand by means of which the True Self pretends that it is not the ultimate reality and therefore not wholly sufficient? Pretense is the only way accessible to the Being-Which-Simply-Is to hide itself and "not to be." It is an act and, if we want to have an idea of how this is done — which can only be an analogy, after all — we have to go to the human theater where actors and viewers pretend not to be who they really are but some other "made-up" being. That is what theater is metaphysically, and it is the best "window" on what kind of activity the visible universe represents in terms of the Infinite Self or the Godhead.

Within the human theater there is the agreement to pretend something. Is such a pretended world subject to complaint about some "better world"? Or is it, like the universe itself, the best possible?

Certainly the human theatrical world is what it is, as and when it is produced. If the pretending is serious and total, no one complains about it or faults it for not being real enough. The seriousness of the pretending precludes this and, in fact, forbids it. All imperfections, such as bad acting, scenery, acoustics, etc. are ignored — forgiven — for the sake of the production. "Pretend harder" is the reasonable rebuke of any and all critics.

We have noticed that, while the theater is just a theater, it and all its personae — human or otherwise — rest on the base of an infinite reality. This base is real, or is present, though ignored. True, it cannot be *seen* in the physical sense, or otherwise sensed, and therefore this base reality, as I have called it, can be easily ignored. But such ease of ignoring should not be treated as proof of non-existence — a common fallacy. For the base reality is real and present: How could a base for something not be present, after all?

It is not there *because* it must be there: necessity is not a cause of reality; it is a characteristic of it. It is there without any cause. Indeed, what can cause being to be except being itself? Which only means that it causes itself and, in that sense, is uncaused.

Is not this base reality — the one that personae in the theater ignore — the real "Best of All Possible Worlds"? Is it not, to put it another way, infinitely better than the limited world?

Such a question is meaningless unless it is joined to a further question: Better for whom or for what? The base or infinite reality is not suited for theater life. Thus, if such a life is intended, nothing else is better for it — for its purpose. And what is its purpose? To provide an "anti-universe," one so close to nothing that the real one has a contrast to it, enabling it to be relished and loved.

How does theatrical life serve as a contrast to the base reality? Precisely and to the degree that the base reality is ignored and therefore made to seem not to be. It is as though the whole of reality is present on the stage, as though no one was supporting Hamlet but that he is there autonomously, as sufficient to himself. "Scientific" attempts would be made to account for him materialistically, by means of "energies and forces and laws" acting blindly beneath the surface. Which is to say that the stage reality is accounted for by grounding it in some "deeper, invisible reality" — just as unexplained and in fact explained less well. In what way intelligence, for example, arises from matter, atoms, forces, etc., is not answered by such scientism.

To "wake up" in the theater means for the activity of focusing on theatrical reality (and therefore of ignoring the base realities) to be terminated. This is the death of the theater or, expressed biologically, the death of the body. But in both cases, what dies does not involve any real dying. Death is merely the end of limitation, of the confinement to a certain place, or space, the waking up to real, non-theatrical existence. Death is an "absolute" only to those who reduce reality to theatrical existence, who do not merely ignore it.

For the theater-goer the best of all possible worlds excludes the end of the theatrical experience — ideally it would go on forever, delivering its reality to the concentrating consciousness. Expressed another way, terrestrial man would then never have to die or to undergo any of the death-echoing traumas of real life.

This is just another way of saying that the appetite for a "better world" is simply the resistance to waking up, the will to continue ignoring the Great Reality which lies at the base of limited, theatrical reality.

The awakening will come soon enough. Death will arrive, but it will not be the imaginary death of limited consciousness, the end of everything, the screen fade-out, the ringing down of the final curtain. It will be the shedding of the mask of the persona, and the resumption of the eternal role of absolute subjectivity, the return to the Great Reality whose hidden presence supported every gesture, every speech, every plot and counter-plot, every pain and every pleasure which took place in the theater of the mind, which is terrestrial existence.

Chapter 18
HOW TO BE
MORE catholic[1]
THAN
THE POPE

Something there is that doesn't like a wall.

— Robert Frost

We live, it is said, in a universe. This word, presumably, is not idle but labels something real, something cohering in unity.

It would seem, however, that the universe is divided, fragmented, split into an untellable number of pieces. Cosmically the galaxies are spread across awesome distances, and hurrying each second further away from each other. Within the galaxies, countless suns, planets, satellites spin in their separate orbits and, as far as is known, have no vital communication between them. On this planet there are divisions within divisions wherever one looks: in the natural order between the animate and the inanimate; in the cultural order with endless divisions of race, religion, color, nationality, ideology, and social circumstance of all kinds. Diversity seems to be a more deeply established fact than universality. In the universe, so-called, there seems to be no one kind or class of things, no uniformity (oneness of forms), but an endless number of different kinds of things, a real pluriformity. There seems to be no oneness about the universe, no inclination of kinds of things to become other kinds of things. Rather everything is doing its utmost to remain what it is, whether it is an apple tree or a dog, a plant or a person. What is more, nations, religions, and innumerable other human groups hold on to their identities, if necessary, to the death. "I want to be what I am," everybody and everything seems to be saying with utter seriousness and finality.

Surely it is insane to struggle against this vast tide of diversity, to try to press things toward a unity which is resisted with implacable force, to challenge the deep-down habit of everybody and everything to be itself. Yet human history is the record of essentially nothing else. It is true that humans usually have not been so foolish to require brutes or inanimate things to become other than what they are (we are told that King Canute had the sea whipped to teach it a lesson about his majesty); but, toward their own kind, they have been merciless. When Egyptian met Hittite, Persian met Mede, or Roman met German or Gaul, there was the effort to change him by slaying, enslavement, absorption. Where believer met unbeliever, whether Christian, Jew, Moslem, Hindu, whatever, there was the sight and scandal of difference and the effort to deny its reality by one device or another, frequently cruel and bloody. Napoleon would have made a host of nations into one nation, a Europe with one coinage, one postage, one code of laws. He collected a great military force to achieve this purpose and left a bloody trail of corpses across Europe.

No, the world is not and will not be stripped of its diversity. All efforts to that end, not just as they concern the hard diversities of nature, but the "soft" structures of human sociology in all its important aspects, appear now as enterprises in the class of that of Canute, vain and insane. Reversion to the older form of things, after "conquest" has done its best to change those forms, is a commonplace of human experience. In human affairs, as in all other things, it must be said, "The more things change, the more they remain the same."

Diversity is for all that, however, an attitude of the eye. The eye sees trees, lakes, mountains, people, planets, diverse things. The mind's "eye" sees nations, religions, races, cultures. Neither eye, the physical organ, nor the "seeing" of the mind, perceives what is also there to see — the reality that all beings have. The universe truly lacks uniformity, riddled as it is with a limitless number of kinds of beings, yet it does not lack another kind of oneness, a genuinely basic and necessary kind, *a oneness in being*. Thus it is a universe in the most successful and meaningful sense of all — in the respect that it, every part of it, is *real*. Consider: What part of the universe is not real and in that respect not like every other part? Indeed this reality is so pervasive that it extends even to those parts that are not "out there," like seas and stars, but which are entirely mental in being. Mental yet real, for they are, after all, more than mere nothings.

It is the *reality* of the universe and nothing else that makes it a universe for, clearly, all else is diversified, radically and unquenchably so. Or to put it another way, it is the reality of the universe upon which its universality must rest. Reality alone can generate a universality which is not a contradiction in terms, because reality alone has an unfragmented, undiversified unity.

One approaches the Scriptures with the greatest reverence and gravity, mindful of their sacred character. Still, one approaches seeking honestly to understand what the writings have to tell us. We come upon those mysterious words of Christ spoken to His disciples: *That they may all be one, as thou, Father, in me, and I in thee.* (John 7: 21). One asks: Was this not a prayer by Christ that His followers share His vision of mankind's unity of being, rather than a charge for them to overcome the legitimate diversities of human culture? Did Christ not *really* say, "That all may be *seen* as one, even as I *see* You and Me, Father, as one?" No doubt it has often been understood by most Christian leaders in the first way, as a challenge to convert the whole world to a uniformity of theological view and even of liturgical practice — a hopeless and frustrating task, as western ecclesiastical history has shown, given the adamantine devotion and loyalty of humans to their long-established cultures.

It should be obvious now how to be "more catholic than the Pope" — as the expression goes — so long as any Pope (or any other religious leader) sees his mission as the converting of non-conformists into uniformists, rather than the educating of all humans to see the established fact of the real unity of the race with the whole universe and with the Godhead.

The latter is done by declining to suppose that anything real is less than real — by having an intellect open to the wonder and mystery and sufficiency of reality, rather than a mind which is forever cutting it up into little packages of thought, the better to "deal with it."

> The King and the Pope together
> Have sent a letter to me;
> It is signed with a golden sceptre,
> It is sealed with a golden key.
>
> The King wants me out of his eyesight;
> The Pope wants me out of his See.[2]

117

Chapter 19
WHAT <u>REALLY</u> MATTERS?

"Well! I've often seen a cat without a grin;
but a grin without a cat! It's the most curious thing
I ever saw in all my life."

— Alice

It is truly amazing how deep materialist prejudice runs in conventional society, sparing not even the elite body of scientists, educators, and professionals in all walks of life. A simple question put in any classroom, from the primary to the graduate level, as to what it is in the blackboard (or universe) which makes it real, brings the unhesitatingly unanimous response: "It has matter." Indeed there is little else on which so many people with any pretense to an education agree in Western society.

But are things real because of their matter? Is it a fact, true beyond reasonable doubt, that the great Western consensus about matter and reality is scientifically secure? Let us see what happens to such a "fact" when it is looked at differently.

There is a famous Shinto shrine at Ise in Japan which is remarkable in its approach to the problem of preservation. In fact it may be unique. Every twenty years the Ise shrine is dismantled and meticulously reconstructed out of new materials specially selected from the imperial forests of Kiso. The last reconstruction, the sixtieth, took place in 1974; the first of which there is documentary evidence was in 685.

Westerners (and perhaps some Japanese) might mock such a restoration. "Restoration, indeed!" it might be said. "All they have at that shrine is a copy, however faithfully done." The view is that if the matter doesn't survive, there is no survival at all. By the "matter" is meant the original wood, stone, metal, whatever. It doesn't count if the form or design survives.

One is strongly tempted to ask at this point: Why doesn't it count if the form alone survives? Isn't that "something," after all? Can there be a shrine, or for that matter (notice the word "matter" here!) anything at all, unless there is a form or design or shape?[1]

No, the reply comes — but still, if you haven't got some matter to work on, all you have is an abstraction, an idea, a mere potential.

To which the response might be: If you haven't got some form or design, however minimal, all you have is a chaos of materials, a heap.[2] In fact since a heap has some order, too, the very notion of a thing without some arrangement of parts, however crude, is contradictory. Which would mean necessarily that material things are collections of designs piled upon each other, beginning with the most infinitesimal things, whatever they might be called.

It would appear then that what really "matters," in the sense of what really materializes, is the arrangement, the form, the design. Paradoxically it is just this "nothing," this "element-that-doesn't-count" in many people's eyes as far as a *true* preservation of the antique object is concerned, that *does* matter, that *does* materialize.

Trying to preserve very old things can be at a certain point as difficult and as frustrating as trying to tie up a pile of sand with a rope. The sand won't cooperate by staying put. Nor will the decayed wall of an old building. The wall and inevitably all the matter in the building will have to be replaced. Obviously, material preservation makes more sense if it is the Pyramids of Egypt. Unfortunately not everyone's ancestors were so cooperative and helpful to the preserving hands of future ages.

Preserving the form exactly, is not nearly so difficult. In fact that is what all preservation ultimately is, although when it is done piecemeal, one small replacement at a time, this is not perceived. The preserver is working under materialist assumptions. Let there be too large a single material replacement and, however faithfully and meticulously the design is preserved, there is a materialist outcry of "Fake!"

Actually, there is really no way to preserve the matter of a material object. It is a fallacy to think that there is, a sentimental illusion kept alive by materialist philosophy. Once one has affirmed that what is real in the world is its "matter," consistency demands, of course, that one insist on the preservation of that which is "real," the matter. It is not a good position to be in, if one is charged with the practical task of preserving the matter in some historical treasure for future generations.

Clearly the Shinto shrine preservers are doing something that makes the most practical sense, saving themselves a lot of frustration and, as a bonus, preserving their important shrine-building skills. They build with materials (wood) solid enough to retain the design for a socially convenient unit of time, twenty years, convenient in the sense that they are able to catch their breath between reconstructions, and yet not so long that the necessary skills will be lost. And then, just when the matter begins publicly to "show its age," that is, when it is no longer able to maintain a decent marriage with the immaterial designs/arrangements/structures that constitute it, the priests of Ise rescue their sacred designs and reembody them in new materials. And all, I am sure, without any apology for what they do, all without any sense that they are not preserving what is most real.

Intelligent preservation, indeed any kind of preservation at all, involves the effort to keep what is most real in existence. This involves focusing on the form of the thing. And when an attempt is made to focus on the matter, because matter is nothing without form, why, quite predictably and naturally, "nothing matters." Or, another way to say it, "matter nothings." Accordingly and predictably, the materialist enterprise fails; or rather it succeeds, when it does, under a false banner, by sneaking formal restoration in inconspicuous doses under the materialist nose. Thus appearances are saved, but as is so often the case with appearances, an illusion is perpetrated.

Chapter 20
HOW TO BE A REAL NOBODY

My whole life consists in the escape from the ignorance that there is a death.

— Robert Graves

If there is one expression in the language which must be viewed as the ultimate insult, the pejorative which dims all others in personal attack, it is that of labelling someone "a real nobody." The phrase is most fascinating in its damning power and surely deserves a close examination.

Here the word "real" is intended for emphasis, to insure that the person in question is not confused with some merely dubious or probable nobody. Once that is settled, attention is directed to the nobody characterization.

Nobody. It is a word that needs to be looked at in its two parts to appreciate fully what is being said. It is simply that the person has no body. Oh, he might look like he does, but really it is just an appearance. Or perhaps though he has a body, he doesn't deserve to have one because, you see, he *is* a nobody. If he hasn't lost his body really, the insult is intended to strip him of it, reducing him to nothing.

Well, what is so remarkable about that, you may ask. Isn't it obvious that when someone loses his body he immediately becomes a nobody? Yes, but what is not so obvious and remains unproved is this: That in losing his body he should be reduced to nothingness. At best it is an assumption — obviously a materialist assumption.

Anything which has a body — a tree, a cat, a man — is real; this is agreed. Does it follow that *only* bodied things are real?

Such an inference doesn't hold water, first of all, at the level of logic. This is best seen when we try to convert, that is, to switch the subject and object of a sentence about which our experience is more complete. If one says all cats have tails, one cannot say all tailed things are cats because dogs and lizards and opossums are not cats. Here we are in a position to avoid a logical error by checking with our experience. In the case of the statement that only bodily things are real, we have no experience to refute it, just the law of logic which says that it doesn't follow as an inference from the true statement that all bodily things are real. Technically speaking the logical error goes by the name of Faulty Conversion. Committing such an error while in pursuit of truth ruins the pursuit: You cannot arrive at truth on the vehicle of violated logic.

Now that we know it is at least possible for some non-bodily things to be real, we are perhaps encouraged to find out if indeed some *are* real. Had we known through logic that they were impossible, clearly it would have been irrational to try to find one. As yet all we have is the encouragement of mere possibility.

At this point I am not so much interested in proving that there is at least one real thing without a body as in pointing out that calling someone a nobody, even a real one, can hardly be as bad an insult as is usually supposed. This is because there is at least the *possibility* that that certain "nobody" exists without his body, that is to say, is truly a *real* nobody. Here the language can get a little tricky, but it need not defeat us if we remain calm.

Clearly, if what is intended is to insult a given person who is viewed with such supreme metaphysical distaste as to regard him deprived of his very being, the pejorative "he's a real nobody" doesn't do it. This is another one of those times when one is tripped up by materialist prejudices, or at least influenced by a prevailing materialism, and led into error. Thus the characterization, "he is a complete non-entity," a phrase that does have some currency, seems a much safer bet. I say "seems" because there are insuperable metaphysical problems connected with any real being issuing into complete nothingness (becoming a non-entity) no matter how powerful the propelling force, for reasons which we will presently see. For the present, the losing of one's body occupies our attention.

If it is a body loss we are talking about, there is a familiar and sure way to achieve it: by dying. A man is driving down the highway, alive and well. Suddenly a truck crashes into his car head-on and he suffers a fractured skull, dying in the ambulance which is rushing him to the hospital. Upon arrival the victim is pronounced dead and his body is removed to the morgue. We are apt to say that the man has lost his life, but we would be on safer ground to say that the man has lost or shed his body. There is simply no evidence that the man has lost his life — this is a materialist assumption — but only that a body (a corpse) has been left behind. Thus it would make more sense in the light of a hard-nosed use of the facts before us to say the victim has shed his body (becoming a nobody) than to say the victim has died. Of course one might accurately say that the man's *body* has lost its life; but that is a lot different from saying that the *man* has lost his life — unless one *assumes* that the living man and his body were identical. And what is the objection to saying that? Simply this: There is then no way to distinguish the man before the crash from his corpse after it. One is obliged to say they are equivalent states of reality — a statement too absurd to merit attention.

Dying is a way of leaving your body behind — of that we are absolutely certain. And language should express, if possible, that which our experience tells us is certain, rather than that which has no basis in experience at all and therefore lacks all certainty. Death is not an event which necessarily destroys a man's life, *as far as we know from the event itself*, but is a process in which a body is left behind by a dying human being, or in which a *body* loses its life. Period.

Now you may protest that I am merely playing with words; that the important thing is that a death occurred, and all the fine philosophical talk about it will not bring the man back to life. Failing to do that, you say, the discussion is a waste of time.

Yet surely such a protest is mistaken, betraying a fundamental ignorance about the nature of human grief. If becoming a real nobody (dying, shedding one's body) involves the certain reduction of the loved one to nothingness, belief (for it cannot be knowledge) in that occurrence brings with it a pain which is necessarily different from the pain of someone going away, an experience which we learn to bear almost every day of our lives so far as our loved ones are concerned.

Therefore to say to someone that his wife and children have died is an unnecessarily cruel way to describe such deaths, cruel *because it says more than the facts of common experience testify,* unnecessary because it doesn't need to be put that way — habits of speech and/or strong materialist prejudices to the contrary. Surely human suffering should be mitigated as much as possible consistent with the truth. And the truth of death is that it is, as far as we know from the evidence which the senses can gather, a process of shedding a body, a process in which a body loses its life. To say other than this, more than this, is cruel, unwittingly if it is done through ignorance, sadistically so if it is done through remediable prejudice. Prejudices which are not warranted by sense experience, particularly those that are inimical to human happiness, are worse than useless; they are anti-social.

Language should not be arbitrarily cruel — cruel, as it were, in anyone's mouth, not just a misanthrope's. It is one thing to be hurt by someone who sets out deliberately to do it, quite another to have it done by a friend whose aim, which is to console, is defeated by materialist language. Try as he might to assuage the grief of his stricken friend, the very meaning inherent in the words "I am sorry that your wife and children lost their lives" cuts the hearer to the quick. How much kinder — and more accurate — is the remark confined to losses that are verified: their bodies. Were the *lives* of these people lost? Where is the evidence that they were?

Who can point to any gain in using materialist prejudices about the act of dying? Neither truth nor compassion are served. That people lose their bodies in death is empirical fact; that they also lose their lives is pure hypothesis, unverified and unverifiable.

Let us turn now to the pejorative remark, "He is a complete non-entity." We have said it "seems a much safer bet" than the "real nobody" characterization. But we meant it only relative to the latter. It must now stand on its own two feet in the light of both logic and human experience.

First, logic. To say somebody *is* a complete non-entity involves one immediately in contradiction, for one is affirming that someone *is* something, in this case a complete non-entity, and at the same time that he is nothing. Logic would require the characterizer to say he is *not* a complete non-entity, which is the exact opposite of what is intended. Here logic is paying its rent to reality for, since there is no way that a being can both be and not be, there is equally no way that one can successfully state such a proposition as that second pejorative. So logically it turns out not to be such a safe bet after all.

Now as to human experience. Just as the sight of a severed arm prompts the judgment that the arm is "dead," so may the sight of a stilled human body prompt an equivalent judgment about the death of the body. But how about the man whose body it was? Is he dead, as well? Perhaps, but *there is no evidence of it*. To say so is a pure, unsupported assumption.

But, you object, a man's survival of the loss of his arm is proved by finding him still existing. Where is the proof that a man who loses his whole body survives?

To which the answer is: Where is the proof that he doesn't? Indeed if a man who loses his arm never survives with his lost arm, all that can logically be said is that a man who loses his whole body never survives with his body. This of course means that he will never be found on the earth, since it is only his body that can be seen. But one cannot logically go from the obvious truths that a man never survives with his body if he sheds it, and that only the body can be seen, to the proposition that not being able to see a bodiless person proves absolutely that he does not exist.

The second pejorative characterization, calling some objectionable person a "complete non-entity," thus fails both at the level of logic and in terms of what experience can corroborate. If it seemed to be a "safer bet," a more viable insult, than the label "real nobody," it was just an appearance; a close inspection of what it implies renders it meaningless.

Persons *may* survive the loss of their bodies — there is a growing body of clinical testimony being gathered by thanatologist-physicians like Elisabeth Kubler-Ross and Raymond L. Moody that in fact they do.[1] But this is and must remain hearsay evidence except to those who come back from clinical death. Their reports do not constitute scientific knowledge since they cannot be publicly verified. Yet they are corroborative and supportive of a position one is permitted to take even without such corroboration, namely, that it is possible that persons do survive the loss of their bodies; that one can indeed become a real nobody. All one has to do is die.

Chapter 21
COSMIC
BIRD-WATCHING

The ignorant get caught in words like an elephant in the mud.

— Lankavatara Sutra

A bird sits outside my window on a branch as I write. It is a pretty finch, a male, its red feathers contrasting with its dominant brown. Its sweet song reaches my ear, and I pause from my typing to listen. Marvelous, I think. More than that: miraculous.

Who or what is this tiny being? I know so little of myself, a human; what does it know of itself? Nothing perhaps, yet it is sufficient in every way unto itself. To me it is a bird. Just a bird? One of countless millions? I refuse the thought; I will not be cheated by numbers — or allow the sense of wonder about my little visitor to perish because of an accountant's squint.

By what supreme magic came it to be a bird, alive with its tiny brain and heartbeat, a master of organic flight, seeing, breathing, balancing, singing? I focus my eye on a single feather on its wing and remember what I know of the great laws of physics and chemistry, the mind-boggling infrastructure of lesser parts that it implies. Who or what are you, little creature? I ask again. Then, almost as though he heard me and could not bear my impious questioning, he is gone. I am left alone to ponder my own questions, refreshed by the experience and emboldened to think there is indeed an answer.

Dare I suppose that among the many powers of divinity is that of assuming the reality of my finch? If it is a crude pantheistic error to think so, as the theologians of the great Western religions warn, what kind of error is it, I wonder, to suppose that divinity has *not* such a power? For what is theological error if it is not the assertion that divinity's power is bounded, that it does not and cannot be at its pleasure a finch?

"Become a creature?" say our theologians. "Impossible!"

But why impossible? Why, if the power of divinity is boundless, could it not be used to become a finch? Because the finch is a creature? Because the Creator cannot be His creature, this involving a contradiction?

The objection rests on the *assumption* that a finch is a "creature." Here one is reminded of an old nursery riddle which asks:

> If you call a dog's tail a leg, how many legs does it have?
> Five.
> No, still four. Calling a tail a leg does not make it one.

And calling a finch a "creature," however emphatically, does not make it one; that is, it does not lift the assumer's burden to prove it is one.

One has but to look to discover that of two assumed possibilities — a finch is either self-creating and therefore divine, or caused and therefore a creature — a finch is unmistakably — the latter?

But why?

Because a finch is finite, limited in its being, mortal?

Granted the divine being cannot *actually* have those characteristics, yet is it not possible, given the divine powers, to *seem* to have them?

Yes, but why would divinity want to do that?

To which I say, that is divinity's business. Perhaps it is for divinity's entertainment. And if you admit that divinity is at least as capable of producing illusion as any good cinematographer, your earlier objection to God as a finch collapses utterly.

Yes, but possibility is not actuality. I haven't proved that God is a finch, even if I have established that God can be one?

It is not my purpose to prove that divinity is a finch, but simply to show the unwisdom of asserting that the finch who graced my window sill is *just* a creature, and therefore *is not* divinity.

Surely there is a gain in seeing possibility where none was seen before. Surely the shift from seeing things only one way, to realizing there can be another way must be called a liberation. No doubt there is satisfaction in the security that comes from nailing things down firmly and finally. Well, at least *that* is taken care of, one murmurs with relief.

And yet there is a price you must pay for such relief: The satisfaction quickly become self-satisfaction, smugness. Now you *know* what that beautiful experience was: It was *just a bird. Just a finch.* Just a creature.

Yet, is it possibly more than this?

No, it is just a bird, a finch, a creature.

It is "just a." This is the awful sound made by the closed-down mind, a mind which is just a mind — a thinking, categorizing, conceptualizing tool — rather than a knowing, feeling, intuiting intelligence. For Hitler, certain human beings were "just Jews;" for Napoleon, the slain on the battlefield of Borodino were "just soldiers;" for some High Inquisitor, a poor, terrified, defenseless human being was "just a heretic." And how can humans who are "just this or that" expect to be treated? The history books contain only the partial record of the consequences of humans who have firmly and finally made up their minds. And what of the non-human world? The record there is even more dismal: many species obliterated, habitats destroyed, whole ecosystems damaged perhaps beyond repair.

The "it is just a _____ " (fill in the blank) attitude clearly is ruinous, not only to knowledge but to its very possibility, a far more serious situation. It can be called an act of deliberately setting traps for the intelligence into which one then confidently walks in the belief that something good will result. And no doubt once entrapped, once the intelligence has been converted to a mind thinking its own products, there is a feeling of safety, of being rescued from the wide and threatening terrain of uncategorized nature. It may be a prison, but it is warm, determinate, and familiar.

Then, from this redoubt one is emboldened to look out through the windows of consciousness, categories-at-the-ready, and to say firmly and finally what anything and everything is. Thus the finch is just a finch, no more, no less.

And if a finch or anything else came as a solitary, utterly independent unit, just as the thinking mind experiences it, then indeed, would mere anarchy, to quote Yeats,[1] be loosed upon the world. For the finch could not fly from its nest, the tree which harbors that nest and the ground which holds and nourishes the tree, the sky which frames it and sends it rain, the planet, the solar system, the galaxies, the universe itself, would each be isolate instead of interconnected by a vast and intimate contract in reality. If, indeed the universe were the way the thinking mind perceives it, and the way the human who is the captive of that mind declares it to be, there could be no universe at all.

And once that prison has been fashioned, once one is utterly persuaded that things are just what the conceiving mind says they are, what then? Particularly if the mind's confinement is experienced as a rational place, a scientific place, and what is more, a place where no troubling or chilling winds of uncertainty blow, a comforting and comfortable place?

It is one thing to be confined by sentencing and punishing forces exercising authority over you from the outside; quite another to be self-confined. Then there is no sense of sentence, no pang of punishment: the mind which has worked to produce that condition now works to lubricate it, to make the subject at ease in his confinement.

What then for the prisoner in the Chillon of his own devising? As he looks at the finch, there is no song or flight of it, no nodding of its bright head, no pecking at its insect quarry which can prompt the wonder of its wonderfulness. It is just a finch. It came by brute, unknown, and unknowable forces, and it disappears the same way. It evolved. Period. Next question.

And yet as high and stout as are the walls fashioned by the conceptualizing mind, a breeze over those walls, a snatch of blue sky through a peephole of consciousness can, if really felt or seen, dissolve in an instant that gilded trap, bulldoze it all into momentary dust. Let us now see how.

It is the mind that refuses the possibility of things being wonderful, of a finch being more than just a finch, indeed much more, of being somehow everything at once (which is, of course, divinity). But let the intelligence come into immediate and unfiltered possession of that finch (or of wind or bit of sky) through sense contact, and in that contact and for however long it lasts, possibilities come to life in the consciousness like dry fields after a drenching.

So let us look at our finch not with our mind but with our wide-open intelligence. For where mind can find only its own conceptions, undoubtedly finite and creaturely, an intelligence using the full power of intuitive awareness will discover reality and its infinite (divine) possibilities, which is really the discovery that our finch is considerably more than just a finch.

The rejoinder you will now want to make is no doubt this: If our finch is not just a finch, its finchness must be an illusion, indeed "just an illusion." Have we escaped one "put-down" of a thing only to stumble into another and perhaps more compromising one?

Not exactly. We should not say of the cinematographic effect of images on screen that it is "just an illusion," that is, it really isn't happening. This is because the images *are* happening; they are not an illusion, or even "just an illusion." The events they portray are imaginary events, pretending to be nothing other than that. True, a given viewer and perhaps an entire audience may cognize the imaginary events as real-order events and be thereby deceived. At which point a friendly reminder from a more informed viewer that "It is only a movie, after all," may provide relief. It may also provoke resentment because the viewer in question may prefer not to remember the truth about movies, in order to enjoy a good scare or cry.

No doubt a subtle point is being made here, yet it needs to be made. The correction regarding Pauline's imminent peril on the railroad tracks is a recall to real life, to life outside the moviehouse. Not so the correction of our narrow view of finches. For when we begin to see a finch as more than just a finch, indeed as (possibly) divinity, we are then in a position to realize it was never "just a finch" in the first place; that it only looks that way to an unenlightened eye. Thus, in our view of the finch we have the reverse process of our view of the heroine at the movies: the image is no more than an image, while the finch is much more than a finch.

Now you may be stirred up enough to point out that if God can assume the aspect of a finch, surely divinity may assume the aspect of Pauline at the movies. The point is well taken. There is indeed no contradiction in such a possibility (as there would be if divinity tried to assume the reality of a square circle.) Accordingly we should be just as careful not to call our Pauline "just a movie heroine." The enlightened human sees the whole universe, movies included, as literally The Scenario of God.

Chapter 22
COSMIC SLEIGHT OF HAND

God's omnipresence is His camouflage.

— Anonymous

In order to succeed at his illusions, the magician must engage the attention of his audience *here* in order to enable him to do his trick over *there*. He must learn the fine art of doing two things well at once, a difficult art which requires a long training. The magician's hand must learn to be quicker than the viewer's eye.

There is no way that the rabbit can both be and not be in the hat at the same time. But there is a way in which it can be in the hat at some subsequent moment, placed there by a magician who, artfully distracting the viewer, introduces the rabbit by a masterful sleight of hand to the surprise and delight of his audience.

It is a case of educating the audience to believe firmly that things are a certain way: without that, there is no surprise, no opportunity to yank the rug out from under the viewer's "solid" expectations. To pull a rabbit out of a hat has no magic value, unless the emptiness of the hat is clearly displayed beforehand. Once the viewer "knows" the way things really are, he becomes committed to it, fixed on it — which is a matter not of mere physical vision but of mental affirmation.*
He is now ready to be fooled.

The human knower now "knows" how things are, is ready to apply the appropriate category, to classify things correctly and to be done with them.

---

* His normal experience conditions him to such an affirmation: Once he puts his key in his pocket, he knows it will not be home on the dresser.

The magician would hardly be discouraged by this state of affairs — it is ripe for his magic. He has an audience set in its mental habits, sure of the way things are, disbelieving that any real magic is possible, thinking: What can he show us that we do not already know?

The answer to anyone who has been to a magic show is: plenty. At a good one, incredible things happen before one's unbelieving eye.

But one does not have to go to a magic show to encounter the magical — it is all around us in nature. If we take commonplace objects like tables or tigers, we encounter one reality at the sense level and, if we are to believe the physicists, an entirely different one in the realm of the submicroscopic.

The mind boggles at the very idea that an object is not, say, a table at all, but a vast collection of hyperactive atomic particles, consisting mostly of space and of incredible relative distances between their material points. The word "illusion" springs naturally and inevitably to mind as one tries to cope with what is being proposed.

There obviously must be some magic — shall we call it sleight of hand? — going on in the universe, some "hand" producing an effect at one level, like an empty hat, and at another level, another "hand" producing an atomic "rabbit."

Surely, there is some illusionist, some magician at work in the cosmos who produces these wonders. But where is he? He seems not to be present.

The situation according to human perception is this: There are everywhere instances of reality, but no Grand Reality itself; magical activity, but no Magician who can be perceived and credited. There is (or must we say, *seems* to be, because we now know there is magic at work, that there are illusions operating) a stage with no Central Performer — just a cast of "poor players" who have their moments of life and being, and then are gone:

> Out, out brief candle
> Life's but a walking shadow, a poor player
> That struts and frets his hour upon the stage
> And then is heard no more.

There is a sleight of hand going on in the cosmos, but it is too swift for the terrestrial eye to catch, too subtle for the human brain to fathom. It is not just the movements of the hand that escape the observing eye — it is the hand itself which is invisible (and, of course, the magician as well). The Cosmic Magician is so skillful that the analogy from human experience with performers of magic is hopelessly inadequate. And yet, analogy or not, it is the one that seems best to describe the situation in which humans find themselves vis à vis the universe in which they live.

The cosmic illusion clearly is multi-tiered, complex, rich. It is an illusion-within-an-illusion. Magic hardly describes it. There are really no words, no human categories that do it any kind of justice. That is why it must be experienced outside of categories, that is to say, mystically. When the mystic, Meister Eckhart, says, "The eye with which God sees me is the eye with which I see God," he is stating a truth about cosmic sleight of hand in words which try to describe something basically indescribable in human experience, something ineffable. Humans know what an eye is, but what does it mean to speak of God's eye, and especially, of God and humans using the same eye for seeing? How does God see with an eye, indeed how does He see at all?

In the sleight of hand that is the cosmos, the table and the tiger are what they are and something else besides. What else? Because each *exists,* they are something more than the *kind* of thing they are: Each is a *reality.* As a reality, there is nothing more for it to become and thus, as such, it is totally everything. How can that which is everything become a kind of thing? By a cosmic sleight of hand which causes the "rabbit" of finite consciousness suddenly to be in the "hat" of terrestrial existence.

The "rabbit" of the Cosmic Magician, who Himself is present so perfectly as to be unseeable, is the man or the dog or the tree or the lake or the stars in the firmament. These are all magically produced from a "nothingness" which is itself a wonder. How is this possible? Ask the Magician, if you can find Him. He is so busy hiding from His audience and even from Himself — that, if He let Himself know who He is, He would wake up from His performance, and the wonderful show that is this world would be over.

What the audience does not know is that it is also one of His "tricks." Indeed, the skill of the Cosmic Magician is so great, His magic so marvelous, that He not only tricks the audience into thinking it is merely the audience, but also, incredibly, He tricks Himself into forgetting that He is doing all the tricks, including the Greatest Act Itself: *that He is not Himself.* The Magician is so skillful *He is His own illusion.* And what can be more magical and more full of wonder than that?

Chapter 23
GOD
AND MAN
AT PLAY

I was with him forming all things . . . .
playing in the world: and my delights
were to be with the children of men.

— Proverbs, 8:30-31

Consider the words: *My delights were to be with the children of men* — they say that God's creation delights Him. How delightful it is that God takes delight in His creatures; without it I think it safe to assume they, including all members of the human race, simply would not be! Surely if creation were not a delight but a drag, God — given the divine foresight — would never have created in the first place, or would have already recoiled from involvement in it. Admittedly, I say "surely" from a human experience with delight extrapolated to the divine. But, then, isn't everything any human can say about God taken from purely human experience?

We creatures are delightful to God! Some of us may not care for bugs and snakes and other "ugly" creatures, we may not give a second thought to hacking away at trees or mountains, or we may even be involved in racial bigotries and self-hatred, yet clearly God loves and delights in creatures, otherwise none of them could be! Surely there is a measure of security we can all feel about our existence, backed up as it is with God's delight!

Nor does one ask: Why does delight delight? The question simply makes no sense, whether asked about human or divine delight. The proper response to such a question is: Who cares? Delight is its own justification; it needs no defense, rationale, or logic. It is an end unto itself.

Yet, paradoxically, delight is serious business. Let it be absent from human activity, whether in fact or anticipation, and no one in his right mind will say, "Who needs delight anyway?"

It would seem, then, that delight cannot be reduced beyond the following: a) delight is its own justification and b) delight is a necessary accompaniment of happiness, and this both for God and man. The activity which spawns delight is not hard to name: It is play.

Play should never be confused with work, although in practice one's work can become play, and vice versa. What decides the matter is whether the activity in question delivers a certain special ingredient, delight.

It makes no sense at all to say that a person *must* play; we say that rather of work, something one must do to earn a living, or which one is drafted, committed, or enslaved to. For work, payment of some kind is expected, precisely because delight is not its purpose. Play, in contrast, is something a person *wants* to do because delight is anticipated.

Work is often experienced as hard and onerous; play as light and effortless, and this even though as much, or perhaps more, energy is expended at it. The person who plays four sets of singles tennis frequently does more "work," defined as weight carried through a distance, than a coal miner over the same time. The tennis player, taking notice of his wet brow and aching muscles, is even apt to say, "That was some work-out!", a remark which salutes at least the superficial resemblance play can bear to work, while assuaging at the same time a bit of guilt felt about playing in a work-a-day world. Still, it is a long way from the work-out to work, as both the player and the worker know.

Play or work, then, is not at all a mere matter of the expenditure of physical effort, but of the end or purpose provoking the effort. The professional who must play his sport for a living is not playing at it, whatever may appear to the onlooker. Which is not to say that his work is innocent of enjoyment and delight. Indeed his very skill guarantees that these qualities are present.

And here we come to the inner heart of play. Play is one of the chief means we have of divesting ourselves of ourselves. This can be seen in the games we play which are all variations on the base-game, "Hide-and-Seek," that activity of infinite delight to children. Only to children? When the skilled golfer swings his club and sends the ball on a high, straight arc to the green, the onlooker marvels at the effortlessness of it all. So many variables gathered up in one smooth, graceful movement! How does he do it? Even the golfer doesn't know! And *this* is precisely his delight. What he does so splendidly, so professionally, he has forgotten how to do!

> For a skill is mastered to the degree that it is "othered," that is, to the extent that it is handed over to unconscious functioning and does not appear to be something that "I" am doing.[1]

Practice and still more practice have caused his skill to drop out of his conscious mind. The skill is his; he is the direct, personal beneficiary of it, yet he has precisely "let go" of it. His skill is a game of "Hide-and-Seek" with himself, and the game is play, and the play is delightful. What he has, in a way, he doesn't have; what he does, in a way, he doesn't do; what would be a burden, if the issue were mere physical effort, is not a burden. What he is, in a certain way, is hidden from him; and in such hiding, there is delight.

There is perhaps no final answer to the question of why play delights. Is it in the pretending? The assumption of the task to be done by unconscious processes? Is it the dispensation from work? Is it any or all of these? Or perhaps others not mentioned? Yet, who cares? It is enough that play delights.

Still one wishes to understand the dynamics of play and of delight.

Clearly it is not only the skilled-at-play, the trained professional who knows delight; for the youngest child takes to play like a seal to water, a born professional. Instinctively the child knows what to "do" with swings and hobby horses, puppets, and toy soldiers. A proposal to play means more to the child as child than to any other in the range of human experience. And putting away the things of childhood, a most forlorn event for humans, means putting away not only toys and games, but the first and most instinctive human activity.

Of course, the activity of play is never really put away for keeps. The desire and need to play, like some enduring refrain of music, keeps returning. Humans are animals who play.

Yet such a statement is narrow: kittens and cats, pups and dogs, calves and cows play as well. Birds and bees play. And who is to say that plants and trees, wind and water, planets and suns, indeed, the whole cosmos does not play? Who will say, finally, that God, Himself, does not play?

When one carefully examines the notion of God-at-play, the subject of the divine necessities immediately come to the forefront. For if the first postulate of the science of God is that His existence is necessary, surely the next postulate has to do with His existence. Thus the argument: If God is necessary to Himself, He is His own end, He is irreducible and Self-justifying. But the important question for us: Does He *work* at His own self-existence or *play* at it? It is one or the other. If He *works* at it, surely it is but a drudgery and a drag, an evil. If He *plays* at it, His existence is — like some divine golfer? — effortless and full of grace, a good. It is, in fact, a delight. His Self-activity must be His happiness, a proposition on which most theologians surely can agree.

Which brings us to another key question: How precisely does God play?

We have seen that the human-at-play engages in some variation of the game-paradigm: Hide-and-Seek. All players actually pretend that they are not themselves. In play they divest themselves (of the weight? the reality?) of their own beings, and the more skilled they become at their play, the more successfully is this done. It is not a real divestment or loss, yet it feels or seems so: it is a pretending.

Can it be that the following propositions are true of God, as well? 1. Creation is a divine activity which is at the heart of God's own felicity. 2. Creation is delightful to God because by it He is able to "lose" His divinity. 3. Creation is divine play. 4. God's creation, the cosmos, is God pretending He is not Himself. Again, Alan Watts:

> . . . God 'others' himself in creating the world, in creating the appearance of innumerable creatures acting on their own. Yet in his own 'secret counsels' the Lord knows very well that there are no others, for 'I am the Lord, and there is none beside me. [2]

Chapter 24
THE
BALANCING
ACT

But what is this universe the porch of
As it veers in and out, back and forth,
Refusing to surround us and still the only
Thing we can see?

— John Ashbery

God, it must be said, is without care as regards the universe. As He is supremely real, nothing can happen to Him which is evil — or, for that matter, which is good, because He is totally and completely good already. The word "God" is tautologous with the word "good."

Yet it would be wrong to say that God is uncaring of the cosmos: The cosmos in its orderly arrangements shows care — careful planning, careful execution. Often it is only from the experience of the occasional oddity, the infrequent anomaly, that the order is even noticed. Thus the comet that falls suddenly and precipitously from the sky comes as a surprise against the background of the vast serenity of the heavens and emphasizes it. Similarly, when monsters or freaks are born, the normal and natural are better perceived.

Humans have a stake in that care for the cosmos, that order, law, and harmony. And when that order is threatened or ruptured, either by natural forces, such as an earthquake, or by man-made ones, such as a war, concern and fear for their safety and happiness arise. Man cares deeply about what happens to him and to his world. He feels that he has much to lose from disorder, not the least his very life. He wants to live, to thrive, to be happy: He is not indifferent to his own fate.

Balance means order. Things out of balance fall, incur damage, damage other things. This explains man's watchfulness over balances in nature, in his own affairs. "Things must not be allowed to go too far," is a sentiment that springs naturally to human lips. And so his eye is on systems that grow too fast (or too slow), that become lopsided in some way, that are out of focus, out of style, out of sorts, etc.

Socially, one must be careful not to go too far, to be *too* patriotic, *too* biased, whatever. The bigoted person is faulted basically for his extremism, for an attitude that represents an imbalance in him and tends to generate it in others.

Seeing an imbalance, we move instinctively to the other side in attempt to correct a situation we deem dangerous. We move more quickly and more fervently when the imbalance is not in our favor, it is true. Involvement tends to obscure the imbalance or makes us slow to see or to admit it. Frequently we insist to the bitter end that there was no real imbalance, that it was all lies, made up by those who were trying to benefit by criticizing or creating panic.

There is a part in each of us that wants the balance tipped over entirely in our favor, that wants the whole pie, would love things to run on forever, provided they went "our way."

We want a balance especially when there is danger that we will be denied, kept from our needs and wants. We then quickly sound the alarm, shouting that things have gone too far.

In soberer, clearer-headed moments we appreciate and favor balance for its own sake. We see that though there is an immediate loss to us, the end result will be a gain and we go along with it. This is our True Self breaking into consciousness, enabling us to recognize that balance and order are the way things must be.

We want ourselves — our side — to win, and we want it at minimum cost. But, if we want to win, we also want it to involve some resistance, some struggle, some competition. Otherwise the victory is boring, and boredom is an unacceptable cost. A state of eternal equilibrium in which nothing is ever disturbed, ever threatened, would not be paradise but a kind of hell of inertia and passivity. No, as Alan Watts has observed about the moral order, "Evil must always seem to be losing but never to lose; good must always seem to be winning but never to win." Otherwise perfect equilibrium has been established, and the game is over.

The game is over. What game is that? It is the cosmos conceived as playing field (or theater), where opposing forces of good and evil, of light and darkness, of being and nothingness compete.

There can be no game where there are no forces in opposition to each other. Must they really be in opposition?

Yes, at least enough to have a game, but not too much to destroy the game itself by eliminating the opposition. This involves the fine art of controlled winning, which is winning that leaves open the possibility of future winning, too.

How does this apply to the game of war wherein two sides try to destroy each other? Surely the game of war is different from, say, the game of football.

Even in war the winning and losing are always controlled. There is a profound, usually unconscious realization that the enemy is needed, and that it is better for it to be the stranger than to have it supplied from one's own camp.

And how does the stranger differ from the kin of one's own camp (family, group, tribe, nation)? He lives, you see, on the other side of the river (mountain, sea); his skin (eyes, hair) is of a different color; he worships a different God; uses words that are taboo to us; is wholly given over to barbarian superstitions and practices. Yet is he not the same in what is essential — in human nature? That, you understand, does not count — it only qualifies him to play the game, not to be on the winning side. There *must* be the game, and differences *must* be found and declared sufficient to identify the stranger as stranger and therefore a danger. But what is the greatest danger of all? *That we may be bored.* That we be locked into an unshakeable equilibrium, that we will no longer be able to know and to relish what we have because all opposition, all contrast, have been removed.

Things are in equilibrium, but tenuously so; they must be threatened with subversion, with collapse, with dissolution, with annihilation. They must be in danger from what is alien to them, from what is unnatural, from what is unacceptable, from what is evil. Otherwise? Otherwise, existence un-challenged will have no game to play, no reason to continue, no need to perpetuate itself. It will lapse into complacency and indifference, then perish with boredom over itself.

Yet it is all a game. Nothing is really threatened, nothing is really in danger of collapse or of annihilation. It is all a pretending.

Reality is complete. It is all that can be, all that needs to be for its own perfection. This means that it is in perfect equilibrium, in matchless balance.

Why then, is there a game at all which engaged humans so seriously and involves all of nature in a strife for survival, a competition to prevail?

If it is all a pretending, a game, why the seriousness? It is because the game-as-game is real; but not as more than a game. To be a game at all, it must be played seriously, played to win, the rules and assignments taken as though the outcome really mattered. And indeed it does matter — as a game: The opposing side is really challenging, the players do need to apply mind and muscle to the task of winning by out-running, out-maneuvering, out-guessing the opponents. The prize of victory is valued — triumphantly by the winners, jealously by the losers.

Yet the game cannot really be extended beyond the limits of its purpose, except artificially. The flavor of the contest may linger, the memory of it may be savored and celebrated afterwards, but there is no way to prolong the substance, no way to keep it alive beyond its special limits. The game was necessarily finite: It had a beginning and an end. It cannot be prolonged indefinitely without defeating its purpose. It can be repeated as a new game, a new unit of activity, and thus gain a kind of interminability through succession, but in itself, it is limited. That is why each brave, resounding victory is essentially hollow; why the cheers and the tears, real as they are during the game, soon fade and in retrospect seem extravagant and even foolish.

It might be said that games are finite because all contestants commit only a part of their reality to the game, the part that is finite, the part that is a part, a kind of thing. The rest — the part that is, paradoxically, not a part at all — is not committed, indeed cannot be committed to any mere game. This is the part that cannot really lose anything, because it is not a kind of thing at all — *it simply and purely is.*

It is the whole self which plays, but only the material or limited part which is involved, that is serious about the game, wants to win, hates to lose. It is this part that gains or wins something by competing, by contesting, by warring. But the commitment of the True Self is never made, indeed, cannot be made. The True Self already has everything, has therefore nothing to gain or lose, is above the battle, sees it as an unimportant, essentially trivial, game.

There is a useful analogy here to the actor on the stage. As a self, he doesn't mean what he says, is not really undergoing the experiences that are occurring on stage. This is because the experiences aren't really happening — no one is really being brave or cruel, happy or sad, living or dying. Yet, strangely, through the magic of theater, this is just what the theater-goers and actors are experiencing. One might say that the actors are there only as actors (and the spectators only as spectators). Clearly as actors (and as spectators) only a part of the full reality is present in the theater, despite the fact that each person is fully there in a material sense. And by material here, we do not mean just in a bodily sense. The people in the theater are not mere bodies, mere robots or puppets on a string. They are alive, intelligent, fully human. By material presence I mean a partial presence, a limited reality.

How can a human being be present only partially? There can be only one way, and that is for that being to be only partially revealed. But this supposes that a simple being is more than a particular, bodily, localized materialized presence; that one can see a man, for example, and not see the whole being. True enough and verified by experience: The actor is there on the stage and we see the man who is the actor, but our attention is directed to the actor and his art, not to the man who is acting and his organic, extra-theatrical existence. No doubt without the organic reality, there could not be the theatrical, but it is the second which is dominantly present, which is most real within the theatrical setting. Everyone neglects — does not see — the man behind the actor. The man is there by "virtual presence" — in hiding, so to speak — the way hydrogen and oxygen are "hiding" in water.

There is a broad base of reality out of which every kind of thing — every limited being — emerges or presents itself. How broad? Unlimitedly broad, a reality which is no kind of thing at all, but simply and purely reality. Such reality has no opponents, nothing to challenge it or rival it. It is primary, without a second. It is a total, unlimited presence. To whom and to what is it present? Certainly to itself, but also to everybody and everything. It is in fact the real being of everything that is real.

That means that it is present on stage, although it is only the acting that is consciously attended to by spectators, and therefore only the acting and the actor are seen, are "real." The man who acts is obviously present but somehow vanishes from sight, is "swallowed up," as it were, by the art of the actor.

We are saying that the totality of reality is present in every instance of reality as the support and base of that instance. This totality, precisely because it is a totality, cannot be seen.

Yet we have said that every game or theater is limited; that is, it is precisely the limiting of the game that causes limited beings to be present to its viewers. This means that there can be no game which unlimited beings can play and be revealed as they really are. And it is this fact which leads to the denial of the very existence of such a being.*

In this sense atheism — the denial of the reality of God — is the result of a "game mentality." It is the equivalent in a lower order of experience of denying that actors are more than actors — indeed much more. It represents so total an immersion in the entertaining magic of the game or the theater, that one is rendered blind to any other reality.

No doubt this theater-vision is useful for appreciating acting and theater-going. All serious participants must "squint" and see only the reality set out on the stage by the script.

Yet it is simply not true that all the world's a stage. The stage hides, suppresses, squeezes out the greater reality. It shrinks it down, and, by dramatizing it, makes it into a performance. It materializes it, to put it simply. The world, life, reality are obviously too big, too inclusive, too real. They need to be cut down, which means, to be "staged."

The stage is necessarily a truncation of the totality, a spotlighting of a selected aspect of that totality. Yet though this totality doesn't appear, like the man who is the actor, it is still there on the stage. True, it cannot be seen, but this is predictable given the smallness of the stage: indeed, the whole physical cosmos is not big enough a stage to enable the totality to show itself. *The totality can only show itself to itself.*

Yet the totality is totally present everywhere. Since it necessarily *is* the reality of everything real, its totality is everywhere. This can be stated as a fact, but it is not capable of being seen or comprehended by any human intelligence. It is nonetheless true.

---

*   The logic — all realities must be present in the game or suffer the consequences of being denied existence — is clearly faulty, though widespread.

And because the human mind cannot apprehend the real in its totality, it quite understandably affirms the importance of sensible things, indeed, it affirms their sufficiency and absoluteness. Such things, it is thought, stand alone; they just are. This is an attempt to invest particular things with the actual totality, to fill a vacuum so intuitively abhorrent to the human intelligence. This is the Skinnerian "nothing but" reductionism, affirming a presence which is only bodily and physical. Clearly, such reductionism cannot be reconciled with the deeper presences of the actors in a theater presentation — and of course, Skinnerians do not even try, dismissing the question as "metaphysical," a sure sign that they are totally immersed in their own game mentality and are unable to see beyond it.

The game mentality is essentially a terrestrial, human mentality. It is a mentality restricted not only to games but by games: Without games, there is nothing to do, no reason to continue on with anything. The game should be won but, even more importantly, as we have said, the game must continue.

The totality is always in full equilibrium, in full balance, with itself. Nothing can happen to it: The only thing that can "happen" to the real is what is already real. The real is everything it can be or ever needs to be. It is the Godhead.

It is extremely difficuilt for terrestrial human consciousness to understand this great truth. At best, there can only be a flickering glance, a dim view as in a darkened mirror. Materiality of consciousness, what we have called the "game mentality," prevents it. In this regard, the seers and mystics see most clearly.

The game mentality is the standard consciousness. Its claims to truth are notorious. Yet the real truth lies outside and beyond it. Chuang Tzu said it perfectly:

> Great knowledge sees all in one;
> Small knowledge breaks down into the many.

CONCLUSION

$$e = mc^2$$

— Albert Einstein

Honest prayer is not rooting for your gods to win but for the real God to exist; such prayer never faileth.

NOTES

INTRODUCTION: The Internal Response

The epigraph is from *Mysticism: A study in the nature and development of Man's spiritual consciousness* (New York: New American Library, 1955), p. 10.

1. "In a celebrated address, read twice before learned societies in 1926 but published only posthumously, Carl Becker recalled that he had been told by an eminent and honored historian that an historian had nothing to do but 'present all the facts and let them speak for themselves.'

"He then proceeded to repeat what he had been teaching for twenty years, 'That the notion is preposterous; first because even if you could present all the facts, the miserable things wouldn't say anything, would just say nothing at all.' " See Bernard J.F. Lonergan, *Method in Theology* (New York: Herder and Herder, 1972), p. 203.

2. Arthur Waley, "The People of Tao-Chou," *Translations From the Chinese* (New York: Alfred A. Knopf, 1941), p. 168.

3. "Within this most vicious circle, we obey and defend beings that exist only insofar as we continue to invent and perpetuate them. What ontological status have these group human beings?" R.D. Laing, *The Politics of Experience* (New York: Pantheon Books, 1967), p. 66.

CHAPTER 1: A Look at Equilibrium

The epigraph is from his poem, "The Mistress of Vision."

1. Gregory Bateson calls this consistency a "tautology:" "Left to itself, any large piece of creatura will tend to settle toward tautology, that is, toward internal consistency of ideas and processes." *Mind and Nature* (New York: Dutton, 1979), pp. 227-8.

2. "It is surely the case that the brain contains no material objects other than its own channels and switchways and its own metabolic supplies; and that all this material 'hardware' never enters the narratives of the mind. Thought can be about pigs or coconuts but there are no pigs or coconuts in the brain; and, in the mind, no neurons; only *ideas* of pigs and coconuts." Bateson, *op. cit.*, pp. 227-8.

3. John Cantwell Kiley, *Self-Rescue* (New York: McGraw-Hill, 1977), p. 77.

4. This fact is clearly demonstrated in the early learning of a language. "Adults accept children's syntactical and phonological 'errors,' which are a normal part of the acquisition process. It is important to understand that when children make such errors, they are not producing flawed or incomplete replicas of adult sentences; they are producing sentences that are correct and grammatical with respect to their current internalized grammar. . . .Since each child's utterances at a particular stage are from her own point of view grammatically correct, it is not surprising that children are fairly impervious to the correction of their language by adults, indeed to any attempts to teach them language." Breyne Arline Moskowitz, "The Acquisition of Language," *Scientific American* (Nov., 1978), p. 94B.

5.   See Karl Stern, *Love and Success* (New York: Farrar, Straus and Giroux, 1975), p. 274.

6.   E.E. Cummings, "Now Does Our World Descend," *The New Yorker Book of Poems* (New York: Viking Press, 1969), p. 495.

7.   *Rubaiyat of Omar Khayyam*, Translated by Edward Fitzgerald, stanza 99.

CHAPTER 2: The Habit of Wounding Yourself

The student referred to in the epigraph is Andy Robinson, 20, a former University of Florida junior.

1.   It can only be reflectively.

CHAPTER 3: Troubles

The epigraph is from his poem, "Songs For Two Plays."

1.   See Viktor E. Frankl, *The Doctor and the Soul* (New York: Bantam Books, 1971), p. 88: "The person who tries to 'take his mind off' a misfortune or narcotize his feelings solves no problem, comes to no terms with misfortune; all he does is to get rid of a mere *aftereffect* (italics mine) of the misfortune. By diversion or narcotization he makes himself 'ignore' what has happened — he no longer knows it. He tries to escape reality. He takes refuge, say, in intoxication. . .and so the suppression of an impulse of grief does not annul the thing that is grieved over." A fundamental argument of this book and the pivot on which the whole of Self-Rescue theory and practice revolves is this: That certain realities, viz., beings of the mind *(ens rationis)* do not have an objective or "thing existence," but are functions of specific willed acts of thinking in now time. Dr. Frankl's "ontology," in my judgment, is not grounded in a genuine metaphysics of existence, as indicated by his commitment to psychological error as the most serious. Thus he calls mental entities in now consciousness "mere aftereffects," presuming that beings of the past and of the future are more real. *This is a psychological* — not an ontological — approach to mental aberration. ". . .[E]xistence, when qualified by 'past' or 'future,' means non-existence. The concept of existence, abstracting as it does from temporal occurrence, cannot by itself convey what is meant by existence. Only in a proposition conditioned by the present can the existence or non-existence of anything be expressed — this table exists, the Dublin monument to Nelson no longer exists." Joseph Owens, "The Range of Existence," *Proceedings, VII Congres Interamericain*, p. 46.

For a more detailed exploration of this problem, see W.E. Carlo, *The Reduction of Essence to Esse in a Realist Metaphysics* (The Hague: Martinus Nijhoff, 1962). Also my *Einstein and Aquinas: A Rapprochement* (The Hague: Martinus Nijhoff, 1969).

CHAPTER 4: Staying Sane

The dates of Hui-neng are 637-712. He is said to have realized enlightenment while pounding rice when training on Mount Huang-mei.

1.   Quoted by Nancy Wilson Ross, *The World of Zen* (New York: Random House, 1960), p. 242.

2. "Rigor alone is paralytic death, but imagination alone is insanity." Bateson, *op. cit.*, p. 263.

CHAPTER 5: On Being Aware of Yourself

The epigraph is from "Letter to Thomas Raikes" (May 25, 1835).

1. "[The] 'nothing' which the mystic uses of God is the superlative exaltation of the divine above all 'something'." Rudolf Otto, *Mysticism East and West* (New York: Meridian Books, 1960), p. 128.

2. "A monk, asking for instructions, said to Bodhidarma: 'I have no peace of mind. Please pacify my mind.' 'Bring your mind here before me,' replied Bodhidarma, 'and I will pacify it!' 'But when I seek my own mind,' said the monk, 'I cannot find it.' 'There!' snapped Bodhidarma, 'I have pacified your mind." In Alan Watts, *The Way of Zen* (New York: Pantheon, 1958), p. 87.

CHAPTER 6: The Unencumbered Now

1. On this point see note 1, Chapter 3.

2. "When we relate the past truly, it is not things themselves that are brought forth from our memory — for these have passed away: but words conceived from images of things: for the things stamped their prints upon the mind as they passed through it by way of the senses. Thus for example my boyhood, which no longer exists, is in time past, which no longer exists; but the likeness of my boyhood, when I recall it and talk of it, I look upon in time present, because it is present in my memory." St. Augustine, *The Confessions*, Book XI, Chapter 18.

CHAPTER 7: The Might-Have-Been Miseries

The epigraph is from the poem "To James McNeill Whistler."

1. *Robert Frost's Poems*, edited by Louis Untermeyer (New York: Pocket Books, 1977), p. 223.

2. *Ibid.*

3. *The Snow Leopard* (New York: Viking Press, 1978), p. 246.

4. *Macbeth*, Act 5, Scene 3.

5. "Crazy Jane and the Bishop," *Collected Poems of W.B. Yeats* (New York: Macmillan, 1964), p. 251.

6. John Holmes, "Misery," *The New Yorker Book of Poems* (New York: Viking, 1969), p. 438.

7. Ella Wheeler Wilcox, "Solitude."

CHAPTER 8: Suicide and Other Hangups

The epigraph is from his Essays, III, 3.
1.   By Doris Portwood (New York: Dodd Mead, 1977).
2.   *Ibid.*, p. 112.
3.   *Ibid.*, p. 106.
4.   Edward V. Rickenbacker, *Seven Came Through* (New York: Doubleday, 1943).
5.   John Berryman, "A Usual Prayer," *Delusions, Etc. of John Berryman* (London: Faber and Faber, 1972), p. 62.

CHAPTER 9: The Great Fear

The epigraph is from *Measure for Measure*, Act III, Scene 1.
1.   *Nicomachean Ethics*, Bk. 3, C. 6.
2.   See the final sentence of this Dialogue: "Now the hour to part has come. I go to die, you to live. Which of us goes to the better lot is known to no one, except to God."
3.   *Op. cit.*, p. 20.

CHAPTER 10: Being Bored

1.   John Milton, "On His Blindness."
2.   William Blake, "Auguries of Innocence."

CHAPTER 11: Living Your Real Life

The epigraph is from his poem, "The Truce and the Peace."
1.   Actually the law only holds if the moving body continues to *exist*, a feature which nature takes care of so dependably and unobtrusively that scientists feel no need to add this crucial metaphysical qualifier to Newton's law. Here Etienne Gilson's point should be remembered: "Physics is that very order of substantive reality in which existence is taken for granted. As soon as existence is not longer taken for granted, metaphysics begins." *Being and Some Philosophers* (Toronto: Pontifical Institute of Mediaeval Studies, 1952) p. 166.
2.   Theodore Roethke, "In a Dark Time," *Today's Poets*, op. cit.

CHAPTER 13: On Good and Evil

The epigraph is from "Samson Agonistes," line 1745.
1.   See Joseph Campbell, *The Masks of God: Occidental Mythology* (New York: Viking Press, 1964), pp. 334 ff.
2.   Alfred Lord Tennyson, "Morte d'Arthur," lines 408-10.

CHAPTER 14: God's Predicament

1.   Alan Watts, *The Two Hands of God* (New York: Collier Books, 1978), p. 30.

2.   *The Myth of Sisyphus and Other Essays* (New York: Alfred Knopf, 1955), p. 56.

3.   At least with the same care that Yahweh defined His nature to Moses in *Exodus*, 3, 14.

4.   More correctly, the Principle of Contradiction which states that, logically, an argument is valid if and only if to assert the premises true and the conclusion false involves a contradiction; ontologically, that a thing cannot both be and not be at the same time in the same respect.

5.   Francis Thompson, "The Hound of Heaven," *Poems* (London: Burns and Oates, 1912), p. 54. See also Gerard Manley Hopkins' poem, "Thou Indeed Art Just," in *A Hopkins Reader* (New York: Image Books, 1966), p. 82.

6.   F.D. Reeve, "The Falls," *The New Yorker Book of Poems* (New York: Viking Press, 1969), p. 221.

7.   K. Kohler, *Jewish Theology* (New York: Macmillan, 1923), p. 176.

8.   St. Augustine of Hippo, *The Confessions* (Chicago: Great Books of the Western World, 1952), p. 42.

9.   A recent philosopher has put it this way: "If the world *is* really simple in containing only relatively few kinds of things and processes, all of which can be connected into a unified level under a single set of laws, it is difficult to explain why it should appear to have the many-dimensional diversity and complexity reflected by the existence of so many different cognitive levels." John Cowperwaite Graves, *The Conceptual Foundation of Contemporary Relativity Theory* (Cambridge: MIT Press, 1971), p. 22. See also my book, *Einstein and Aquinas: A Rapprochement* (Martinius Nijhoff, The Hague, 1969), especially Chapter 3.

10.   See his *Mysticism: Christian and Buddhist. The Eastern and Western Way* (New York: Collier Books, 1957), p. 63.

11.   *Ibid*, p. 61.

12.   *Ibid*, p. 65.

13.   St. Augustine, *Confessions*, X, 30.

CHAPTER 15: Weeping With One Eye

The epigraph: This is Mr. Burns, the actor.

1.   "The irritable individual becomes less irritated not simply because will-agency keeps him from it, but because he develops other attitudes which, by the alchemy of psychic process, discourage irritableness." Peter Bertocci, "The Moral Structure of the Person," *Review of Metaphysics*, March, 1961, p. 378.

2.   "Jesus Laughing," *God's Images* (New York: Seabury, 1977), un-numbered.

3.   "Little Gidding," *The Four Quartets* (New York: Harcourt, Brace & World, 1943), p. 59.

CHAPTER 16: God As Movie Director

The epigraph is from *Twelfth Night*, Act III, Scene 2.
1.   Muriel Gardiner, *The Deadly Innocents: Portraits of Children Who Kill* [preface by Stephen Spender] (New York: Basic Books, 1976).
2.   John Ashbery, "Robin Hood's Barn," *Self-Portrait in a Convex Mirror*, (New York: Penguin Books, 1976), p. 62.

CHAPTER 17: The Best of All Possible Worlds

1.   "The occurrence of every event, past, present, or future, signifies. . .a definitive realization, permissive in the case of sin, of the divine plan, to which, in the decree of the divine wisdom, no amendment of a more desirable nature can exist or be possible." Pierre Conway, O.P., "Possibility and Divine Omnipotence," *The New Catholic Encyclopedia*, Vol. 6, p. 630.

CHAPTER 18: How To Be More catholic Than The Pope

The epigraph is from "Mending Wall."
1.   From the Greek, *katholikos*, meaning "universal in extent; involving all or having sympathies with all; liberal; broad-minded: to be *catholic* in one's tastes, interests, etc." *Random House Dictionary of the English Language*, (New York: Random House, 1966), p. 234.
2.   Charles Henry Webb, "The King and the Pope."

CHAPTER 19: What *Really* Matters?

The epigraph is from Lewis Carroll, *Alice in Wonderland*, The Complete Works of Lewis Carroll (New York: Random House, 1976), p. 74.
1.   "If an elephant had the dentition and other formal characters of the *muridae*, he would be a mouse, in spite of his size. Indeed, the cat-sized hyrax is close to being a hippopotamus, and the lion is very close to being a pussycat. Mere size seems to be irrelevant. Form is what matters." Gregory Bateson, *op. cit.*, p. 203.
2.   ". . .Tables are not *just* collections of molecules. . .The organization, the wholeness, the specific identity, or what Aristotle would call the form of the table are what do not appear at the level of molecules." John C. Graves, *op. cit.*, p. 24.

CHAPTER 20: How To Be A Real Nobody

1.   See Elizabeth Kubler-Ross, *On Death and Dying* (New York: Macmillan, 1969) and Raymond Moody, *Life After Life* (New York, Bantam Books, 1977).

CHAPTER 21: Cosmic Bird-Watching

1.   See his poem, "The Second Coming."

CHAPTER 22: Cosmic Sleight of Hand

1.   William Shakespeare, *Macbeth*, Act. IV, Scene 5

CHAPTER 23: God and Man at Play

1.   Alan Watts, op. cit., p. 23.
2.   *Ibid*, pp. 23-24.

CHAPTER 24: The Balancing Act

The epigraph is from "Self-Portrait in a Convex Mirror," op. cit., p. 77.

SELECTED READING

Adler, Alfred, *What Life Should Mean To You* (New York: Capricorn Books, 1958.) Adler: 20th Century Aristotle. Neurosis as vanity.

Aristotle, *Ethics.* Full of insights about human nature, unchanged after 25 centuries.

Carlo, William Ernest, *Philosophy, Science and Knowledge* (Milwaukee: Bruce Publishing Company, 1967). Wisdom about many things by a medieval scholar and master teacher.

Fowles, John, *The French Lieutenant's Woman* (Boston: Little Brown and Company, 1969). A "metaphysical novel," beautifully written.

Bateson, Gregory, *Mind and Nature: A Necessary Unity* (New York: Dutton, 1978.) A bold "summing-up" by an eminent anthropologist with a profound grasp of scientific method, if not always of ontology.

Berkeley, George, *Three Dialogues Between Hylas and Philonous,* ed. by Colin M. Turbayne (Indianapolis: Library of Liberal Arts, Bobbs-Merrill Company, 1954). How real is matter? Let Bishop Berkeley tell you all about it.

Illich, Ivan, *Medical Nemesis* (New York: Bantam Books, 1977). A brilliant book that may change your thinking about medical progress.

Kiley, John Cantwell, *Self-Rescue* (New York: McGraw-Hill Book Company, 1977). The first in a three-part series with one still to come.

Laing, R.D., *The Divided Self* (Middlesex, England: Penguin Books, 1965). Is the soul, possessed by transcendent longings, "insane," or simply struggling toward a higher state of mental health? Laing, a British psychiatrist, defends a valid mysticism based upon a religious sensibility which is not a Freudian illusion.

Lilly, John Cunningham, *The Scientist: A Novel Autobiography* (Lippincott, Philadelphia, 1978). The incredible odyssey of a pioneer physician in the domain of interspecies communication.

Maritain, Jacques, *The Dream of Descartes* (New York: The New York Philosophical Library, 1944). Maritain writes passionately about the mathematical "mysticism" of Rene Descartes. An eye-opener.

Matthiessen, Peter, *The Snow Leopard* (New York: The Viking Press, 1978). A beautifully narrated account of a journey of 250 miles in the Himalayas by a skilled observer and a determined inner searcher.

Merton, Thomas, *Asian Journal* (New York: New Directions, 1973). The posthumously edited journal of the renowned Trappist monk who died in Bangkok while on tour. A modern odyssey of a God-seeker.

Moody, Raymond, *Life After Life* (New York, Bantam Books, 1977). A trained philosopher with a medical degree who has taken seriously the testimony of persons who returned from clinical death. It may change your mind about oblivion.

Morris, Ivan, *Madly Singing in the Mountains* (New York: Harper Torchbooks, 1972). An appreciation and anthology of the remarkable Orientalist, Arthur Waley.

Murphy, Michael, *Golf in the Kingdom* (New York, Viking Press, 1972). A fascinating book about a Scottish mystical golf master by one of the founders of Esalen.

Peck, M. Scott, *The Road Less Traveled* (New York: Simon & Schuster, 1978). A brilliant book by a psychiatrist who has broken out of the purely "medical model" approach to mental illness. It will gain a wide, respectful audience.

Penfield, Wilder, *The Mystery of the Mind* (New Jersey: Princeton University Press, 1975). A world-famous neurosurgeon arrives at some remarkable conclusions about the nature of the human spirit. Technical but readable.

Plato, *The Gorgias*. The story of what happened when a sophist took on a master philosopher. Exciting and enchanting reading.

Rickenbacker, E., *Rickenbacker* (New York: Prentice-Hall, 1967). Autobiography of a man who survived, among other things, twenty-three days on a raft in the South Pacific.

Roszak, Theodore, *Where the Wasteland Ends* (New York: Doubleday, 1972). A masterly study about the consequences of the breakdown of transcendence in human society.

Selzer, Richard, *Mortal Lessons* (New York: Simon and Schuster, 1976). A book by a surgeon/poet about his experiences.

Trungpa, Chogyam, *Born in Tibet* (London: Allen and Unwin, 1966). The autobiography of a reincarnated lama who led his people out of Tibet in the dead of winter during the Chinese takeover of his country. A truly remarkable document.

Walsh, John, *Time is Short and the Water Rises* (New York: Dutton, 1967). The story of a remarkable wildlife rescue operation in Surinam. Contains a hair-raising account of a long swim at night across a piranha-infested lake.

Watts, Alan, *In My Own Way* (New York: Pantheon, 1972). The autobiography of an English philosopher turned American who interpreted the wisdom of the East in dozens of important books.

—————————, *The Two Hands of God* (New York: George Braziller, 1963). A classic exploring the myths of polarity by a modern theologian-philosopher who writes like a poet.

INDEX

A fantastic representation of the universe from an early
sixteenth-century woodcut. The man is thrusting his head
through the starry firmament into infinity.

"I do not insist that my argument is
right in all other respects, but I would
contend at all costs both in word and
deed as far as I could that we will be
better men, braver and less idle, if we
believe that one must search for the
things one does not know, rather than
if we believe that it is not possible to
find out what we do not know and
that we must not look for it."

— Socrates in the *Meno*